Women

Who
Charmed
The

West

WOMEN WHO CHARMED THE WEST
by Anne Seagraves© 1991

Other non-fiction books by Anne Seagraves:

Soiled Doves: Prostitution in the Early West: ©1994

High-Spirited Women of the West: 1992

Women of the Sierra: 1990
Second Printing: 1991
Third (revised) Printing: 1992

Tahoe Lake in the Sky: 1987

Beautiful Lake County: 1985

Women
Who
Charmed The
West

By Anne Seagraves

Published by WESANNE PUBLICATIONS
Post Office Box 428
Hayden, Idaho 83835

Library of Congress Number 91-065794
ISBN 0-9619088-2-3

ACKNOWLEDGMENTS

Arizona, University of, Tuscon, Arizona; Buffalo Bill Historical Center, Cody, Wyoming; California State Library, Sacramento, California; Harvard Theatre Collection, Cambridge, Massachusetts; The Historic New Orleans Collection, New Orleans, Louisiana; Lake County Library, Lakeport, California; Lake County Museum, Lakeport, California; Nevada Historical Society, Reno, Nevada; Nevada State Library, Carson City, Nevada; Ohio Historical Society, Columbus, Ohio; San Francisco Performing Arts Library and Museum, San Francisco, California; San Francisco Library, San Francisco, California.

While researching *WOMEN WHO CHARMED THE WEST*, many individuals have been extremely helpful. The author would like to express her appreciation to these people.

Donna Howard, Curator, Lake County Museum, Sandy Frey, Lake County Library, Lakeport Branch; The staff of the California State Library for their outstanding cooperation in obtaining old newspaper articles and portraits; Elizabeth Holmes and Tina Stopka, Buffalo Bill Historical Center; Particia Aker, Photograph Curator, San Francisco Public Library; Laurie Ratliff, San Francisco Performing Arts Library and Museum; Jessica Travis, The Historic New Orleans Collection; Ruby Glebe, Lakeport, California.

AND A VERY SPECIAL THANKS TO:

My husband, Wes, for his many hours of research, and Louise Talley for walking with me every step of the way. And to the wonderful editors: Wes Seagraves, Louise Talley, and Dave Stoneberg.

The first public amusements and early days of the theater have always fascinated the American people. From its beginning, entertainment has represented a jumbled array of talented people who were scattered through time like priceless gems. Many were never recognized; a few became legends.

The American theater was established in the early 1700s, when a few of the less puritanical colonies attempted to produce plays and entertainment. Since the first American colonies consisted mostly of Puritans, Quakers, and Lutherans, they frowned upon anything that was superficial or trivial. Many times the leaders would stop or impose a fine upon those attempting to entertain, calling the performance "painted vanities."

Following the American Revolution, George Washington, who had an interest in the theater, took part in amateur plays and attended New York theaters. Because of this, laws were soon repealed and tolerance for entertainment grew.

The acting profession was not respected, however, and the colonists felt that most actors were immoral and all actresses lacked virtue. Due to these beliefs, players in the early theater usually married within their own profession. Their children were also forced to become entertainers; there was little else they could do. New York and Philadelphia were the only early cities with fewer restrictions; their mixture of races and people made them more liberal.

The first plays were Shakespearean, and most of the performers were from Great Britain. Many became wandering entertainers who moved from place to place putting up their own makeshift buildings, since there were no theaters. The early plays were translations of English origin, later followed by melodrama, romance, and realism, many of which were written by local authors.

A few of the early Western theaters to be built were in Nashville, Tennessee; St. Louis, Missouri; and in New Orleans,

Louisiana, where the famous French Opera House was completed in 1859. In 1847 William Chapman appeared upon his "Floating Theatre," and the Eagle Theatre in Sacramento, California, was built in 1848. The first theatrical performance by professional actors in California, however, was given in San Francisco at the National Theatre in 1850.

Stock companies were formed with traveling stars who visited the principal theaters of America. They usually had a hustler who went ahead to put up billboards and place advance notices and advertisements in the newspapers.

Respectable women of the early 1800s would not be seen in a place of entertainment, but by 1850 a few daring females began to appear in theater audiences. In the 1860s the rules of society changed, and women were no longer considered to be immoral if they attended a theatrical event. Unfortunately, this did not pertain to actresses, who didn't receive respectability until the early part of the 20th century, and even then, many of the "proper" ladies frowned upon them.

As the need for entertainment grew in the frontier communities, medicine shows took to the road along with traveling minstrels. The performers traveled by foot, riverboat, and stagecoach. They had to be strong and dedicated because life was demanding, with makeshift lodgings and seldom a hearty meal.

In the 1870s the variety shows appeared. They offered everything from cheap, bawdy fun to acrobats, singers and comedians with slapstick. The floors were covered with sawdust, and the seats were hard. When the audience became excited, they would hiss the villain, applaud the heroine, and cry for the downtrodden.

Vaudeville soon followed, and the star system was born. Entertainment and the theaters improved, with more refined performers and one-act plays. The theater was finally recognized as legitimate, and the world of entertainment has continued to prosper and grow ever since.

Throughout this publication the author has spelled theater two different ways — theatre, when it was part of a proper name, and theater, for the general text — both are correct.

To the remarkable women of the theater —
The entertainers of
yesterday —
today, and tomorrow —

"I've seen lovlier women ripe and
real, than all the nonsence of
their stone ideal."

— Byron

CONTENTS

Cover Photo: Maude Adams
Courtesy California State Library
Graphic Artwork: Julie A. Knudsen
LaserType and Graphics

The actresses in this book are legendary. Tales of their personal lives are so interspersed with fact and myth that the author carefully researched stacks of material to hopefully find truth. Many of these talented ladies were famous throughout the world, some only in the United States. They all contributed to the theater and each story is different. From the Victorian era of the 1800s through the turn-of-the-century, famous stars like Lillian Russell, Sarah Bernhardt, Maude Adams, and Lillie Langtry provided the real glitz and glitter of yesterday's entertainment world.

Life was not easy for these ladies, but they were dedicated to their profession and willing to make sacrifices. All of them were overworked and many suffered nervous or emotional breakdowns. The stress of playing the same role for several years, or constantly changing characters and plays, was demanding.

Transportation was limited. An actress in New York who wanted to appear on the West Coast either journeyed by wagon across the plains, traveled over the dangerous Isthmus of Panama, or took the perilous trip by sea around Cape Horn. There were few sanitary facilities. With the arrival of the railroad in the late 1860s, life became a little easier. Some of the more prominent stars enjoyed the luxury of a private Pullman car; the majority, though, used the common coach.

Their careers revolved around New York, which was recognized as the theatrical capital of America. Its flashy variety houses, elegant theaters, and sophisticated audiences were a large draw. In the East, however, ladies of the stage were still considered, by women, to be immoral or "sinful." Society matrons would stand in line for hours to see an actress perform, but rarely invited her to a social event or to enter their homes.

It was in the frontier towns and cities of the West that these talented artists were received with friendliness and respect. Since San Francisco paid the highest wages, it became known as the theatrical capital of the West. Almost all of the famous actresses appeared in that city and, while playing there, they not only entertained the audiences, they charmed them!

Most of the actresses in this book did not appear on the movie screen. The few who did usually resembled flickering shadows which did not pay tribute to their beauty and talent. Although there were recording devices, they, too, were immature.

One can only imagine the dramatic voice of Sarah Bernhardt or the golden tones of Lillian Russell. In the end, it was the written word that recorded the stories of these fascinating women.

It would be impossible to write about all of the famous stars of yesterday. However, there are a number who reached the top of their profession and remained there long enough to be recognized; among these few are *the women who charmed the West.*

As you turn the pages of this book, let the curtain rise in the theater of your mind, while these remarkable women of the past stroll silently across the stage of time.

―――――― ◆ ――――――

In order to write this book,
the histories of many distinguished women
have been researched, along with numerous
newspaper articles and reviews.
As in all biographical material,
fact and myth are interspersed. I have
carefully sorted through countless pages
to hopefully find the truth.

— The Author

◆―――――――――――――――――――――――◆

Maguire's Opera House

MAGUIRE'S OPERA HOUSE
San Francisco, California

This impressive theater was established in 1856 by Tom Maguire, and could seat 1000 people. The first entertainment consisted of minstrel shows, novelty acts and stock companies. They were followed by famous imported stars from all over the world offering comedy, drama and eventually Shakespeare. In 1859 it was elegantly refurbished and Maguire ventured into the field of opera. Since San Francisco was considered to be the theater capital of the West, most of the famous visiting stars usually played at this opera house.

Theatrical — "This evening we are to have the first theatrical representation in San Francisco. Atwater and Co., of the Eagle Theatre of Sacramento, have leased the building known as Washington Hall, in the rear of the St. Charles Hotel, and have been busily employed in erecting their scenery and setting up the interior for the accommodation of the public. It is to be opened this evening. The company is small, but under the judicious management may be made attractive.

We learned yesterday that a theatrical company from Sydney have arrived consisting of five male and three female performers. We should think it would be for the advantage of both parties to join forces, when they would be able to present pieces in better shape, and be surer of public patronage."

San Francisco Alta, January 16, 1850

◆━━━━━━━━━━━━━━━━━━━━◆

The French Opera House

THE FRENCH OPERA HOUSE
1859-1919 • New Orleans, Louisiana

This handsome structure of the Italian order of architecture had a front of 166 feet on Bourbon Street, 187 on Toulouse Street, and was 80 feet tall at its highest point. When thoroughly packed the auditorium could seat from 2000 to 2500 patrons, though its seating capacity was advertised as 1600.

The entire second floor front of the building contained a saloon and conversation rooms furnished in the most beautiful style. There was an arcade and gallery projecting from the front to provide a shelter for ladies entering and leaving their carriages in bad weather. Its interior was decorated in subdued faded reds, with contrasting creamy whites and gold. There were no bizarre effects of color or lighting to confuse or distract the audiences attention. The atmosphere was elegant and in good taste, filled with serenity and charm. Every consideration was given to insure the comfort and enjoyment of the discriminating theatergoer.

New Orleans was considered to be the musical capital of America, and it was the French Opera House where the famous stars appeared. Noted opera singers, talented musicians, and popular plays of the day were presented at the opera house from 1859 to 1919, when the magnificent building was destroyed by fire. It was said at that time that the heart of the Old French quarter had died with the opera house.

Many associations and dedicated citizens have attempted to rebuild the famous landmark, and although the French Opera House has not been revived, its tradition and charm remain a part of New Orleans historic past.

*Lillian Russell,
as seen in the play
"An American Beauty."*

✦ ———————— ✦

Chapter 1

LILLIAN RUSSELL
✦ ———————————————————— ✦
An American Beauty

L illian Russell was a corn-fed American girl from Iowa who became the ideal of her generation. With her voluptuous figure, high plumed hats, and flamboyant lifestyle, she represented the plush era of the Gay Nineties. Wealthy men like Diamond Jim Brady showered her path with glittering diamonds, as her lovely voice and natural charm carried Miss Russell to the top of her profession.

This famous star of musical comedy, christened Helen Louise Leonard, was born on December 4, 1861, in Clinton, Iowa. Her mother, Cynthia Van Leonard, was a dominant, outspoken feminist who had little time for her five daughters. Her father, Charles Leonard, was the publisher of the weekly *Clinton Herald.*

In 1865, at his wife's request, Mr. Leonard sold his prosperous newspaper and moved the family to Chicago, where he opened a printing firm. The move allowed Mrs. Leonard to devote her time and energy to women's rights and other worthy causes. Little Helen was placed in the Sacred Heart Convent School, where she delighted the teachers with her bright personality and bell-like soprano voice.

Upon her graduation from the convent, Helen entered a finishing school and started taking music lessons. She had reached the age of 17, and men were beginning to notice her shapely, statuesque figure and fresh young loveliness. Mrs. Leonard also recognized her daughter's beauty, as well as her promising voice. She knew there were few opportunities for Helen in Chicago, so in 1878 she moved with her daughters to New York, the theater capital of America, where the young woman could reach her musical potential.

In New York, Helen's mother placed the young woman with a famous voice teacher and embarked upon establishing a career for her talented daughter. Helen's peaches-and-cream complexion, hourglass figure, and startling blue eyes were quite an attraction. Her clear soprano voice could effortlessly reach high C, and everyone, including her teacher, felt she would become a great opera star. Helen, however, had other plans, and one year later, at the age of 18, joined the chorus of Gilbert and Sullivan's "H.M.S. Pinafore."

In "Pinafore," Helen radiated an earthy magnetism on stage that attracted the attention of the audience, especially the men. Flowers and proposals were sent backstage following every performance. Although Helen enjoyed the salary and acclaim, she left the chorus line within a few months to marry the orchestra leader, Harry Braham. Mama Leonard complained in vain as she watched the unhappy marriage fall apart and her beautiful daughter bear a son, who died shortly after his birth. Helen secured a divorce from her husband, not realizing this was the first of many unfortunate marriages and love affairs she would endure. The lovely actress, it seemed, had poor taste in her choice of men.

Following the disastrous marriage, Helen returned to the stage. There, her lissome beauty caught the eye of Tony Pastor, a theater owner and producer who was noted for discovering new talent. Pastor heard Helen sing and immediately placed her on the stage of his Broadway theater as an "English Ballad Singer." He also changed her name to Lillian Russell. As Miss Russell, she went on to appear in a burlesque, "The Pie Rats of Penn Yan," becoming a part of Pastor's traveling troupe on its way West.

In San Francisco the audiences were enthusiastic in their praise of the enchanting Miss Russell. Her appearance in "Babes in the Woods," drove theatergoers wild when she walked onto the stage wearing a pair of purple tights that displayed more than a little of her shapely legs. This was considered quite daring in an era where a naked ankle created a sensation! Repeat performances sold out, and Lillian received bouquets of flowers as well as expensive jewelry. She became the "Toast of the Town," and San Francisco paid her the highest tribute accorded any actress.

Despite the honors bestowed upon her, Miss Russell remained unspoiled and generous; her personality was as gracious and charming as ever.

In 1882, at the age of 21, Lillian decided she was being underpaid by Pastor and returned to Gilbert and Sullivan for higher wages and plays that had more class. Under their direction, she appeared at the Bijou Opera House in New York, where her fresh beauty and lovely voice brought the house to its feet. Unfortunately Miss Russell, who was reaching new heights in her career, again lost her heart to yet another musician. While Mother Leonard argued in vain, the love smitten Lillian eloped with Edward Soloman, an English composer. Soloman coerced Miss Russell into breaking her American contracts, insisting she accompany him to London to appear in his operetta. Lillian left New York behind, along with disgruntled managers, unpaid bills, and, for the first time in her life, bad publicity.

Miss Russell made her debut at London's Gaiety Theatre in Soloman's operetta and, although the audience criticized Soloman's music, they found Lillian's voice delightful. She went on to appear at various London theaters at less than her usual wage, and the couple had to lower their standard of living. Money was scarce and Soloman was working on a new operetta.

That winter Lillian's daughter, Barbara, was born, and a few months later her husband produced "Polly," a successful musical, with Lillian playing the leading role. The couple took "Polly" back to New York, where it was well-received, and Miss Russell began to appear in several musicals and plays of the day.

Although her career was soaring, Lillian was not to enjoy marital bliss. In 1886 her marriage created a scandal that rocked the world when Mr. Soloman was arrested for bigamy. It seemed he already had a wife in London when he married Miss Russell. Lillian received a hasty annulment and, filled with humiliation, she joined J. D. Duff's company on its way to the Pacific Coast, where she appeared in "Iolanthe," and other popular plays.

At this time Lillian was only 25 and had already suffered two unsuccessful marriages. She was still a beautiful golden blonde, but motherhood and a hearty appetite had turned her statuesque figure into something more than substantial. She carried close to 165 pounds on her 5-foot, 6-inch frame and, although a full-figure was considered desirable, Lillian was afraid of displaying too much flesh. When her producer insisted she appear in tights before the Western audiences, Miss Russell politely objected, claiming she might catch a cold and that scanty attire in the smaller towns would surely be met with disapproval. After a considerable discussion, it was unanimously decided that no one wanted the star to become ill or ruin her reputation; Miss Russell did not wear tights!

Lillian Russell was known for her enormous plumed hats and jeweled dresses. She represented all that was glamorous and was considered to be the ideal female of her generation. When she returned from the triumphant two-year tour of the Western United States, Lillian Russell was at the peak of her career. Her reputation was firmly established, and she commanded the highest salary of her profession. With this in mind, Miss Russell decided to negotiate her own salary and asked for an increase in wages at the end of each season. If she was refused, Lillian would promptly find another theater and producer; needless to say, she was seldom refused.

In 1890, at the age of 29, Miss Russell was chosen to be the first person to speak over the new long-distance telephone. On a special line linked from her dressing room in New York to Washington, D.C., she sang a song from the "Grand Duchess." Her clear voice must have been pleasing to the ears of the group of notables, including President Harrison, who were listening on the other end. Her voice was later recorded on one of the first phonograph records; Lillian was then earning $35,000 a year, a very high wage for that day.

Although Miss Russell was America's own corn-fed sweet-heart, she was snubbed by the women in her hometown. It would appear her profession made her notorious; all actresses were considered immoral, and that included Miss Lillian Russell. She was welcome to appear in public, but rejected in private. When she attended the race track (a hobby she enjoyed), the "proper" matrons refused to associate with the great actress. The women at the Washington Park Clubhouse went so far as to request that she be ordered to leave. Lillian, however, had the last word when she was regally escorted to the finest box in the grandstand. During this period Lillian Russell met the famous Diamond Jim Brady, and their friendship endured for the rest of their lives.

James Buchanan Brady was the son of an Irish, immigrant saloon owner. He rose from the poverty of a tenement district to become one of the wealthiest men in America. Brady hated the slums, street gangs, and starvation. He was always considered a "fat boy," and at the age of 11, Brady, who resembled a 15 year old, went to work as a bellhop. When he reached 15, he also started working in a saloon. While there, the young man saw so many alcoholics that he decided he never wanted to drink; and he never did.

Since Brady already knew reading, writing, and arithmetic, he spent his spare time learning how to conduct himself as a polite businessman. He knew that wealthy men were supposed to wear diamonds, carry a watch chain, and speak with confidence. Brady had always loved to eat and, because the meals were free, he ate only the fanciest food. By the time he reached manhood Brady was a large, amiable rich man who, next to food, enjoyed the theater.

Jim Brady dressed immaculately; he was smoothly barbered and always filled with good cheer. There were diamonds on his fingers and a three-carat diamond in his cane. At the age of 28 he became known as Diamond Jim Brady, a man who always had a pocket full of diamonds. Through lavish spending he bought his own popularity, and he was always seen in the company of the popular actresses of the day such as Lotta Crabtree, Lillie Langtry, and Sarah Bernhardt. When he met Lillian Russell, however, all the rest were forgotten. He became her constant companion and showered her with so many diamonds that she became known as "Diamond Lil."

In 1891 Lillian Russell became the star of "The Lillian Russell Opera Company," and opened at Manhattan's Garden Theatre in "La Cigale." Her voluptuous beauty and exquisite voice filled the house nightly. After the performance she would usually join

Diamond Jim for a late supper, where she held her own at the dining table. Jim had a stomach six times the size of a normal man, and his dinner consisted of several main courses, followed by a five-pound box of chocolates and a gallon of fresh orange juice. Jim always tried to leave four inches between his stomach and the table so he could eat in comfort. Reporters, watching the couple dine, described them as "Beauty and the Beast." That didn't bother Lillian, however, she accepted Jim as he was and enjoyed his companionship.

Miss Russell took her company on the road in 1894, when she was 33, and "La Cigale" was greeted by thunderous applause. She was hailed as a true American star whose costumes were American and so elaborate that the *San Francisco Call* wrote:

> *It is pretty generally understood that the costumes worn by Miss Russell in "La Cigale," are novelties and models of the American dressmaker's art, and that despite the dictums of the ancient playwrights ... the styles have never been known until they came into grace on the perfect form of the "Divine Lillian." It is equally well known, too, that Miss Russell has confidence sufficient in her own country's artists of apparel to entrust them with the designing and making of her dresses. It goes without saying, therefore, that when the curtain rolls up on Lillian Russell at the Baldwin, and that accomplished woman faces hundreds of her sex present, it will be found that her confidence has not been misplaced. She will have the keenest critics in dress sitting before her. Women are almost, if not quite, as intent on studying an actress' gowns as in criticizing the plot or the music of the opera. Added interest will be felt too, in that, while the play is of French origin, France can claim no share in the dress creations that will adorn the star. A French opera will be interpreted by an American woman clad in American gowns.*

Is it any wonder Lillian Russell was so loved and that her beauty was described as legendary?

Following the Western tour, Lillian met and married her third husband, co-actor Signor Giovanni Perugini, a smallish man who was a well-known matinee idol. Miss Russell had been single for almost eight years and Perugini completely won her heart. Even Mama Leonard approved as the happy couple were united in a quiet wedding ceremony. Their marriage, unfortunately, did not prove successful. The couple soon delighted the press by attacking each other in public. Lillian claimed she was unloved and that Perugini had never consummated their marriage. She further stated that he was overbearing and had tried to throw her out the window. Perugini stated that off the stage Lillian was too ugly to love and he couldn't possibly throw his wife out a window because she weighed far more than he did! The whole affair was so embarrassing to Lillian that she moved out of the apartment, totally disillusioned by marriage. It seemed all Perugini wanted of Miss Russell was to further enhance his own career; to him, she was just a stepping stone to popularity.

The press showed Lillian Russell no mercy as they ruthlessly tore her life to shreds. They claimed she was a "fallen-woman" who would never be satisfied by any man, and reviewed her three unsuccessful marriages with glee. Some newspapers went as far as to declare that the great actress was incapable of love as well as careless in her choice of mates. In her distress and humiliation, Lillian turned to the one man she could always rely on, Jim Brady. Diamond Jim was living proof that all men were not scoundrels. He was understanding in her time of need and provided an available escort who made no demands. The newspapers soon found someone else to write about, and Miss Russell went on with her life and career without the aid of Signor Perugini; she was also a lot wiser.

By 1895, when Lillian was 34, the well-upholstered men of that period began to admire thinner women. What was once considered a healthy appetite was looked upon as a handicap. Newer, slender actresses were competing for leading roles, and although she was still a top performer, Lillian Russell knew she had to go on a diet. Her weight had reached an uncomfortable 185 pounds and the press began making uncomplimentary remarks about her excess flesh, and her abundant 42-inch bust.

Tired of being heavy, Lillian and Diamond Jim decided to cut back their calories and started looking for a form of exercise. Since it was the era of cycling, that became their choice. Jim had gold-plated bicycles made to order with diamonds on the handlebars. His bike was reinforced to carry his hefty 285 pounds, and Lillian's was enhanced by her monogram in diamonds and emeralds. This strange pair made an outrageous appearance as they pedaled around Central Park, gaudy but happy, and losing weight. The rest of Lillian's life became a constant battle to keep off unwanted pounds—it was no longer a time for self-indulgence—it was a time for survival!

Lillian joined Weber and Fields in their new music hall in 1899. At 38 years of age she was still a top box office draw in America, with a salary to match. The music hall was a unique experience for Lillian. Although she started in vaudeville, it had been a long time since she had appeared in light, fast-moving productions. She was soon dancing and singing in musicals like "Whirl-i-gig" and "Fiddle-dee-dee," and the audiences loved it. In this new and happy field of entertainment Miss Russell's sparkling talent boosted her even higher up the ladder of success. She played in "An American Beauty," and won the hearts of the nation, becoming America's most renowned beauty. Lillian Russell remained with Weber and Fields for six years, touring America, charming audiences, and packing every theater.

In 1906 Miss Russell's throat started to deteriorate, and she had minor surgery. Years before, the great opera star Ernestine Schumann-Heink had warned Lillian to be less generous with her high Cs and to save her voice. Lillian, however, did not listen; she felt the audience had paid to hear her sing, and sing she would.

Following throat surgery, Miss Russell played straight comedy and vaudeville. She traveled thousands of miles in her private Pullman car, appearing in theaters all over the United States. Diamond Jim met her occasionally, and one time he even asked Lillian to marry him, but they both decided their relationship was merely platonic and not one of a physical nature. They would be friends forever, but never lovers.

In 1912, when she was 50 years old, Lillian Russell married

Alexander Moore, owner of the *Pittsburgh Leader*. He was a powerful man in the Republican Party, extremely wealthy, and very much in love with Miss Russell; she finally achieved a happy marriage.

Lillian started writing a syndicated column for her husband's newspaper and became an advocate of women's suffrage. She still appeared in vaudeville, and at one time let her name be used to advertise "Lillian Russell's Own Preparation," a popular cosmetic. In 1914 she starred in her first moving picture, "Wildfire," opposite movie great John Barrymore. The film was unsuccessful, and she turned to the feminist movement, touring the country on behalf of women's rights. Lillian joined in demonstrations and marched in parades. While other younger actresses rode upon horses or in cabs, Miss Russell preferred to walk proudly along the street. It was said she converted more men with her stately carriage than any famous speaker of the day.

In 1918, at the age of 57, Miss Russell retired from the stage. During her farewell appearance the New York theater was packed with standing room only. As the lights dimmed, Lillian, wearing her finest jewelry and an elegant, high plumed hat, majestically made her way from the back of the hushed theater to the stage. As she passed each aisle, the audience rose to pay tribute to the American beauty who had entertained them for so many years. Aisle after aisle they stood, while the great lady of the theater took her place upon the stage. They remained standing as Lillian Russell bid them a final farewell.

In 1922, at the age of 61, Lillian Russell passed away from cardiac exhaustion and was buried at the Allegheny Cemetery near Pittsburgh. With her passing the Golden era of the American theater ended, leaving memories of a happier time and a talented, fresh blonde beauty who had charmed theatergoers for 43 years.

◆ ─────────────────────────── ◆

*Lillian Russell as Patience,
a village milkmaid, in the musical
"Bunthorne's Bride."*

◆ ——————————————— ◆

Lillian Russell as seen in the
chorus of Gilbert and Sullivan's
"H. M. S. Pinafore."

Lillian Russell

The female ideal of her generation.

LILLIAN THREATENED WITH SEIZURE BY SHERIFF

Emerging from her dressing room and standing in the wings of the Broadway Theatre in Brooklyn, Miss Lillian Russell saw a man staring fixedly at her. When she went out on the stage, she could feel that basilisk glare almost piercing her back. When she retired from the view of the audience, there stood the same man with the burning glare. Miss Russell had worn the close-fitting trousers and the swell-hipped frock coat and the shiny silk hat before tens of thousands of eyes in the season of "Whoop-Dee-Doo," but never had she felt as uncomfortable as under the piercing eyes of that fellow in the wings.

"The most impertinent stage hand I ever saw," she said to Fields. "Stage hand?" groaned the comedian. "I wish that's all he was. He's a deputy sheriff and he's attached the costumes."

"Mine?" gasped Lillian. "Yours—all." "Even-even these?" and her beautiful eyes roamed over her lavender nether garments. . . . Then he hastily explained that a firm of theatrical advertising agents, who asserted that Weber and Fields owed them $524, had got an attachment from Justice Garretson on the ground that the comedians had been out of the State for six months and had carried certain property with them. While Weber was pouring out this tale, there was hasty telephoning to J. C. Judge, counsel for the alleged creditors.

"Oh, well," said Judge, "I don't wish to embarrass anybody." (As if Lillian hadn't been deeply embarrassed already). "Tell the sheriff he can wait until tomorrow."

The company heard the joyful news. Miss Russell looked herself over; then stared haughtily at the deputy sheriff.

"Don't wear them away from the theater, please." said he, departing hastily. The performance went on to the end. Next day Weber and Fields willingly paid the bill. . . . But it was noticed Miss Russell, when she went on the stage next night, looked apprehensively over her shoulder and then at—well, at those.

San Francisco Chronicle, May 18, 1904

◆─────────────────────◆

Lillian Russell

*The San Francisco newspapers described her
as "airy, fairy Lillian."*

◆ ————————————————————————— ◆

Lillian Russell

Miss Russell was known as "Diamond Lil."
Wealthy men showered her with diamonds.

Lillian Russell

*Her fresh young charm and lovely features
made her a symbol of her time.*

◆━━━━━━━━━━━━━━━━━━━━━━━━━━━━━━━━━◆

*Although she became
increasingly stout Miss Russell
continued to play to a full house.*

◆ ──────────────────── ◆

*Sarah Bernhardt as
"The Queen" in
Victor Hugo's "Ruy Blas."*

─── 40 ───

Chapter 2

SARAH BERNHARDT
Tragedienne

S arah Bernhardt was a part of the past that today's youth know little about. She was an enchanting genius ... a feminist who wore swirling silk scarves and velvet skirts. Her superb acting ability earned her the title of "Sarah the Divine." A woman of contradictions, she would end a perfect performance by declaring "God was there," while her flamboyant love affairs and unorthodox lifestyle shocked three continents.

Many neighborhoods of Paris, France, have claimed to be the birthplace of Sarah, the legendary tragedienne, who was born on October 23, 1844. Her mother Judith Van Hard was of middle-class Dutch Hebrew ancestry. She was a beautiful courtesan who was called Julie and known for her many lovers. Sarah's father was believed to have been Edouard Bernard, a French Catholic student from the Left Bank. Edouard obviously cared about the child because he left Julie 100,000 francs for her support.

Julie was an ambitious woman whose prime desire was to live in luxury. Since morality was not part of her life, and infidelity was accepted by French society in that era, she became a kept woman. There was no place in her apartment for a child, so Sarah was packed off to the country to live with a nurse.

The home where Sarah spent her childhood was cold and damp, and many nights she went to bed hungry. Since Julie didn't bother to visit her daughter, there was no one to see that the child had proper care. Sarah grew into a thin, emaciated little girl with a chronic cough; the doctors feared she would never reach maturity. No doubt, it was this depressing atmosphere of illness and neglect that helped to foster an obsession with death and an insecurity that became part of Sarah's personality.

Sarah was brought back to live in Julie's apartment when she was seven. By now the unhappy little girl desperately needed her mother's love, something she was never to receive. Julie was expecting another child, her second daughter Jeanne, who was given whatever small affection Julie possessed. Without the attention she craved, Sarah became unruly and hard to manage, so Julie sent her to a special school for young ladies.

The school proved to be a disaster for Sarah who was never trained in social graces. She could not relate to the other girls and soon became an object of ridicule, which made the child withdraw even further from reality. Sarah also developed uncontrollable emotional problems and started having seizures. Neither the school nor Julie could allow such disruptive behavior; so Sarah, who was then 10, was placed in a Catholic convent. It was there the girl received her first taste of love and understanding. She developed an almost fanatical love of the church; and although Sarah became a Catholic, she always remembered her Jewish origins.

At 15 Sarah returned once more to Julie's apartment to live with her mother and two half sisters, Jeanne and Regina. There she met Madame Guerard, a widow who lived in the same building. The lonely girl grew to love and respect Madame Guerard and affectionately called her Mon Petit Dame. Madame Guerard became Sarah's lifelong friend and companion.

The move back to Paris did little to improve Sarah's life. She was jealous of her sisters and attempted to ignore her mother's "sinful" behavior. Sarah considered herself a Catholic and spent many hours pretending she was a nun; she started pulling away from everyone except Mon Petit Dame. Unloved and occupied with thoughts of death, she was mortally afraid of being buried in a plain wooden box. At this point in her life, it is believed the insecure Sarah demanded from Julie, and was given, a rosewood coffin that in later years received much publicity.

By the time Sarah reached 16, she was so dramatic that Julie's friends couldn't tell whether she was acting or not. She would frequently change her moods from sadness and tears to tantrums. Her rolling eyes and wraith-like appearance were confusing. One of Julie's friends suggested that the emotional creature would make a good actress. This horrified Sarah, whose religious background led her to believe that acting was "wicked."

Following many arguments, Sarah attended her first performance at the theater with Julie and was so frightened by the large, noisy audience that she called it the "monster." Once the curtain went up, however, Sarah lost herself in the play. The young girl, who had never belonged anywhere, knew that night her future was the stage; Sarah Bernhardt silently vowed to be the greatest actress the world would ever know.

When Sarah first auditioned for the conservatory of drama, she received no encouragement or affection from Julie. The young woman made her appearance alone, wearing a severe, unbecoming dress. As she looked at the hostile, upturned faces, Sarah, who was terrified, became angry. She defiantly recited her piece with such feeling and emotion that she was accepted.

Throughout the years Sarah spent at the conservatory, and the fame that followed, Julie never gave her love or expressed pride. In fact, her mother's infrequent appearances would almost destroy Sarah's acting ability. She tried so hard to please Julie that she often forgot her lines. During her lifetime Sarah Bernhardt suffered fright many times before the curtain was raised. It was always her pride and the challenge to conquer the "beast" that came to her rescue.

Sarah Bernhardt was known as "Sarah the Divine," "Madame Sarah," "The Bernhardt," and as the legendary "Grand Dame of the theater." Her performances were brilliant. Once the curtain was raised, she became one with the role she played. Her instinct and timing were perfect as she glided across the stage. Sarah spoke only in French to the hushed audience, and she thrilled them ... Sarah never shocked them.

When the play was over, Sarah did not bow for her curtain calls. She would either stand with her hands clasped or stretch her thin arms out in recognition of the people. Tears would fall from her eyes at the sight of the many flowers thrown at her feet. At times she would blow kisses and the band would play the moving strains of the Marseillaise. Her leading man always stood close by her side so he could catch the fragile actress in case she fainted. Together, they would leave the enthralled audience with Sarah leaning gently on the arm of her co-star.

Sarah was a delicate, intoxicating woman who throbbed with energy. It has been said her beauty was like a cloak, she could put it on or take it off as she pleased. Many have described Sarah as being as thin as a bone; it was said her dressmaker used a skeleton as a model for her clothing. When Alexandre Dumas was asked to describe Sarah, he replied that for all he knew she could even be fat! Sarah created her own image: she was believable.

In reality, Sarah Bernhardt was small and graceful. She wore yards of veils and scarves which gave her a flowing, gossamer appearance. Her unruly mop of red hair, that has been described as a bright aureole, surrounded a delicate, pale face with hooded blue-green eyes and thin lips. When Sarah draped herself in furs, she displayed an almost feline grace. At other times she appeared to be in anguish and would throw herself to the floor as though in the throes of death.

Sarah's first lover was a handsome officer in the hussars, Prince Henry de Ligne of Belgium. The dashing prince fell madly in love with Sarah, who at 21 was the toast of Brussels. Their passionate affair ended when Sarah discovered she was pregnant. It has been said the prince loved Sarah and wanted to marry her. His family, however, announced that a half-Jewish actress bearing an illegitimate child was totally unacceptable. So, the prince returned to the hussars, and Sarah decided to dedicate her life to the theater. She left Brussels for Paris to stay with her mother until the child was born, only to find she was unwelcome.

Julie's days as a courtesan were over. She had accumulated a considerable fortune from her profession and gained respectability. When Sarah turned up at her door Julie forgot her own tainted past and ordered her sinful daughter out of the home. Sarah, together with Madame Guerard, rented a small flat.

The following months were difficult for Sarah who had never been strong. She accepted any part that was offered, and somehow they survived. The birth of Maurice Bernhardt in 1865, when she was 21, was one of the greatest moments in Sarah's life. A strong bond of love and admiration between mother and son developed that lasted throughout Sarah's lifetime. Maurice adored his mother; and years later when his father suggested he assume the family name of Ligne, the young man proudly rejected the offer saying, "I am the son of the great Sarah Bernhardt."

Following the birth of Maurice, Sarah went on to become "the darling of Paris." She was completely absorbed in the theater and spent at least 14 hours a day rehearsing, consulting with designers, and studying her roles. Sarah Bernhardt wanted perfection. She instinctively knew if a part was good or bad, and in all her years on stage, never let herself be typecast. Sarah was constantly looking for a new role and new writers. When her relentless professionalism left her exhausted, she had the rare ability to lie down in the middle of the stage and sleep for exactly one hour, awakening fresh and filled with vitality.

Sarah Bernhardt could portray male characters as well as female and was extremely popular as Hamlet. She controlled the audience with her magnificent eyes and expressive gestures. She was glamorous as well as dramatic and had a large repertoire. Sarah gave outstanding performances as Cleopatra and Joan of Arc, but the two plays that made her famous were "Phedre" and the immortal "La Dame aux Camelias," which today is known as "Camille."

In "Phedre," a story of a woman who had incestuous desires for her stepson, Sarah paced the stage wringing her hands with genuine anguish. It was the lead in "Camille," however, that became her greatest role. In this play, written by Alexandre Dumas, "The Divine Sarah" portrayed a fallen woman, a beautiful courtesan who, although dying of consumption, was reluctant to bid a last farewell to her lover. This role provided Sarah with a vehicle to display her own obsession with death. Wearing a diaphanous white gown, she played the tragic Marguerite; and although she appeared in the role for years, Sarah always left the audience emotionally spent.

Sarah Bernhardt's personal life was one of constant confusion. The actress who demanded perfection on stage lived in a cluttered apartment where nothing matched. It was filled with valuable paintings placed beside dead plants. The walls of her famous salon were of red damask covered with Oriental weapons and busts of mythical beings. Her carpet was of thick, red velvet. A canopied bed covered with satin pillows and fur throws stood in one corner, while both wild and domestic animals wandered at will.

The now famous rosewood coffin was kept in Sarah's bedroom. It was lined with white satin and had ornate golden handles, which she pawned whenever the money ran out. Sarah occasionally slept in it so she would get used to death. It has been said that she allowed herself to be photographed in the coffin during several mock funerals. She would cover herself with wreaths and flowers and lie with her hands folded upon her breast. A small glowing candle was placed at her feet. Many of Sarah's lovers claimed to have been entertained in the rosewood coffin.

Sarah's love affairs were considered scandalous. She grew up watching her mother entertain many men and felt it was immoral to arouse a desire that would not be gratified. Sarah was a passionate woman who believed in marriage and fidelity, although she did not practice either. Her name has been linked to such famous men as The Prince of Wales, Albert Edward the VII; Franz Joseph, Emperor of the Austro-Hungarian Empire; novelists Gustave Flaubert and Emile Zola; and dramatist Oscar Wilde, who adored her. She preferred creative men or perfect masculine specimens and never discussed her romances. When the affair was over, the ex-lover usually became her devoted friend.

Bernhardt strongly believed in the emancipation of women and would have made a fine suffragette. She was a liberal and opposed capital punishment, crime, and poverty. She loved animals and flowers and felt there was no such thing as "the tradition." Although Bernhardt could not endure being alone, she seldom arrived on time for appointments or special occasions. Many times she didn't even bother to show up. She never wrote a thank you note, and Mon Petite Dame made all Sarah's apologies. In her own words, Sarah Bernhardt claimed that she seemed to attract all the mad people in the world.

By the time Sarah was 36, her family had grown to include

Maurice, her two half-sisters, Madame Guerard, and anyone else who needed a place to live. She was generous to her friends and lived far beyond her means. In 1880 Sarah, who was tired of constantly being in debt, decided to undertake the first of many tours of the United States. Although she was reluctant to leave her beloved son Maurice, Sarah set sail for America amidst a mass of confusion and tearful farewells.

Her arrival in New York City generated a considerable amount of excitement and curiosity. Sarah's reputation and legends of her numerous love affairs were known throughout the world. She was met at the dock by a noisy crowd of reporters and a band loudly playing the Marseillaise. All of this caused Sarah Bernhardt to lock herself in her stateroom. The frightened actress finally opened the door only after her manager convinced her that no one meant her any bodily harm.

In America Sarah became known as "The Bernhardt." She was to receive $1,000 a performance, plus 50 percent of the gross receipts over $4,000, and her expenses. She did, however, have to furnish her own elegant wardrobe, which was quite costly.

Sarah's notoriety created so much excitement that she packed every theater and again became an overnight success. The news media constantly followed her, reporting her every move. Screaming fans fought for scraps of her scarves, a piece of her dress, or to touch the famous Bernhardt hand. Women started dieting so they could wear a flowing Bernhardt gown — thin was in, and anything French was considered the vogue.

Although Sarah was riding on a wave of success, New York high society did not accept her. She was never invited to their homes or social affairs. Her circle of friends consisted only of men or people within the theater. The ladies would stand in line for hours to see the famous actress, but did not welcome her into their personal lives. She was considered "French," a term that meant her plays were probably "naughty" and that the actress herself was, no doubt, a "sinful" woman. Bernhardt calmly shrugged her shoulders at their hostile attitude, while the box office did a thriving business.

As Sarah moved westward, she acquired "The Sarah Bernhardt

Special," which consisted of three Pullman cars for her personnel and a Palace Car for the great actress. The Palace Car contained her usual menagerie of assorted people, pets, and confusion. Bernhardt would sit on a large platform wearing furs and scarves as she enjoyed the scenery along the route. She lived like a queen and became a familiar sight traveling the country on the Bernhardt Special making one-night stands. Sarah, who had heard of the notorious western highwaymen, always kept a small pistol by her side.

The theatrical troupe visited most of the larger cities throughout the United States. In the West, Sarah was treated with courtesy. She might have been considered a "terror" on stage and a courtesan, but Bernhardt was invited into the homes of the leading citizens. She was recognized as a great actress who, despite the fact that she spoke French, was accorded the honors she deserved.

In 1883, following her first American tour, Sarah met and married her only husband, Jacques Damala, a Greek aristocrat. Damala's handsome face, perfect physique, and nonchalant, mocking charm swept Bernhardt off her feet. During their marriage he had many lovers, participated in wild escapades, and became heavily addicted to drugs. The great Bernhardt, who had never lost control of a love affair, made a fool of herself over the arrogant, insolent Greek, 11 years her junior. Her infatuation was so great that she granted his every wish. In return, Damala spent her money and deserted her for another woman, leaving an empty bank account. Sarah was forced to sell her jewels and go on a European tour to pay his debts.

When she returned from the tour, Damala was back on her doorstep, broke, and in a morphine stupor. Once again he made her life miserable, sneering at her in public, spending her money on drugs, and causing humiliating scenes at the theater. In order to protect her reputation, Sarah was forced to obtain a legal separation and eventually had him put in a sanitarium. Damala was an emaciated, helpless addict and remained a burden until his death in 1889. Julie also died the same year, and Sarah's heart was broken over the loss of a mother who had never loved her.

At this point in her life, Sarah was 45 and very much alone.

Although her relationship with her son was satisfactory, he was not one she could lean upon. Maurice had never learned to support himself, and his fondness for gambling created a considerable financial drain on Sarah's pocketbook. Where Maurice was concerned, however, the devoted Sarah would shrug her shoulders and give him whatever he requested. So, once more the theater came to Bernhardt's rescue as she poured her heart into each performance.

Sarah Bernhardt toured America on and off from 1880 until 1918. Her 1891 tour was quite extensive. She traveled almost all of the United States, visiting the rural as well as urban areas. During that period her appearances in "Camille" earned her the title of "The Divine." Many of her performances were so moving that the play had to be interrupted several times for her to accept the applause. She always left her audience in tears, wanting more.

In her later years Sarah became thick around the waist, but refused to wear a corset. The first lady of the theater, it seemed, was still as lithe and graceful as ever as she floated across the stage, with or without the aid of a foundation garment! She continued to entertain and charm her public long past the days of her youth. The famous Bernhardt always managed to give the illusion of one who was eternally young.

In 1916, due to an injury sustained in the past, one of Sarah's legs had to be amputated at the thigh. Although her convalescence was long and painful, Sarah returned to her life—the theater. The gallant actress who wouldn't wear a corset also refused a wooden leg. Instead, a special chair was designed to carry her to and from the stage. Bernhardt learned to raise her body on one leg so she could stand during her performance when necessary. In 1917 she bid farewell to the United States in her final tour.

Before her death Sarah began appearing in one-act plays and vaudeville and also taught acting. Ignoring ill health and advancing age, she began a series of lectures as well as rehearsing a new play. On opening night in 1923, Sarah Bernhardt collapsed and was taken to her retreat on Belle-Isle-en-Mur, where she received the last rites of the Catholic church before she quietly closed her eyes at the age of 79.

The final curtain had fallen upon Sarah Bernhardt, the great tragedienne who was like no other. She confronted death as she did her audience—only this time she could not conquer the "beast." The golden voice of the Divine Sarah was silent, and the rosewood coffin was placed in a mausoleum in the cemetery of Pere Lacaise, France.

Note: In 1914 Sarah Bernhardt became a Chevalier of the Legion of Honor, the highest award her country could bestow.

Miss Sarah Bernhardt

BERNHARDT NEWS

Bernhardt is a model for those American women (which means all) who are desirous of preserving their youthful energies, even though Dame Nature makes it impossible to hold rosy freshness long past the early twenties. The French woman has just celebrated her sixtieth birthday and has expressed herself emphatically to the effect that she feels as sprightly as when she first went on the stage in 1862. There is a suspicion that enthusiasm has led the actress to indulge in a little exaggeration, but there is a significant lesson in her tireless activity. Eighteen hours a day are given over to her profession. She is nearing the 150th performance of "The Sorceress," and incidentally has found time to rehearse and act twice Rostand's "La Samaritaine." Besides this she has settled down to daily rehearsals of Lavedan's "Marie Antoinette" and has arranged for the early presentation of "Varennes," another drama of the French revolution. Bernhardt goes to the theater six days in the week at 8 A.M. and does not leave for home until 2 A.M. The Paris correspondent of Fiske's publication, the Dramatic Mirror, says the actress is enabled to keep at her tiring task by taking extreme care of her health. Bernhardt's appetite is always on edge, and when work brings weariness she finds renewed strength in eggs whipped in beer. This is a queer concoction, but the actress is a living example of its efficacy.

San Francisco Chronicle May 8, 1904

◆————————————————◆

The great Sarah Bernhardt in 1887,
in the role of "Theodora," a
Byzantine actress and courtesan.

SARAH BERNHARDT IN CALIFORNIA

In 1880 the famous French actress Sarah Bernhardt made her first tour of the United States. Californians eagerly awaited her arrival as she traveled across America, conquering her audiences. Unfortunately, they had to wait seven years to welcome the Divine Sarah, who did not reach the Golden State until 1887, during her second tour.

When the Great Bernhardt finally arrived in Oakland, her private train was met by a frenzied mob, and she was appropriately greeted with a speech from the secretary of the French Dramatic Society. Reporters described her as "not so thin nor so ugly—and much more gracious than they had anticipated." She was then taken in a carriage to the ferry which transported her across the bay to San Francisco.

Sarah complained of the cold weather and confessed to being afraid of the San Francisco audiences, saying she had heard they were very critical and quite demanding. On the evening of her debut, however, the sophisticated, glittering audience was charmed and enthusiastic over her performance. Sarah's simplicity and intense portrayal of her role created an aura of magic. The Examiner described her as "a woman of incomparable charm and intoxicating magnetism." One writer claimed, "She is the greatest actress of all time."

Bernhardt remained in San Francisco two weeks. During that period her repertoire of plays included the popular "Camille." At the end of her engagement, the triumphant Sarah departed for France with a heavy pocketbook, promising to return.

In 1891, on her longest world tour, Bernhardt did return to the West Coast on her way to Australia. Her private train, the Bernhardt Special, was met in Nevada by Sam Davis, a

young writer for the San Francisco Examiner, who reported her escapades and appearances throughout the rest of Sarah's California tours. He described her traveling style as "barbaric luxury" and was overwhelmed by the Bernhardt confusion of bric-a-brac, animals, and assortment of people. As they became friends, Davis learned to share her love of nature and participated in many of her wild pranks.

Sarah's 1891 San Francisco season opened at the Grand Opera House to the usual overflowing, enthusiastic audience. Following the performance, Sarah, with her interpreter and her escorts, toured the twisted alleys of Chinatown. While there, Bernhardt honored a Chinese playhouse with her version of a Chinese play. Her pantomime sent the house into gales of laughter and delighted the audience so much that they pelted her with vegetables. This warm, friendly side of Sarah, that was so seldom seen, made her even more popular with the public.

When Bernhardt left San Francisco, she took 81 cases of champagne home to France and left a farewell note that when translated read: "My heart beats with emotion at leaving this adorable and hospitable city. I cry au revoir to all and thanks to each."

Sarah's return in the fall of 1891 included a visit to Southern California. She appeared in Los Angeles, then a thriving community of 50,000, where she was described by the press as "a strange creature."

In 1901, 1905, and 1906 Bernhardt again toured in America. In 1906, upon hearing of the devastating San Francisco earthquake and fire, Sarah rushed to Chicago to assist in a benefit for the city she loved and raised close to $17,000 for the homeless.

Following the benefit, Bernhardt traveled to San

Francisco to perform; however, there were no theaters left, so she played at Ye Old Liberty Playhouse in Oakland. On May 27, 1906, she appeared in "Phedre" before an audience of 5,000 at the Greek theater of the University of California. The theater was a gift from William Randoph Hearst. In the beautiful outdoor auditorium, Sarah's silvery voice so inspired the refugees from the earthquake that they temporarily forgot their personal losses and terror. She also donated a percentage of the proceeds to relief funds.

With her energy undiminished by time, Bernhardt returned to San Francisco in 1911, when she was 67, for a "farewell visit." She went on to perform in Los Angeles, which by then had grown to a population of 300,000. Sarah continued her tour, which included San Diego and Catalina Island, then headed north for performances in Santa Barbara, Bakersfield, Fresno, Stockton, and San Jose.

Two years later, in 1913, the indefatigable Sarah again came to California. She was 69 years old; and although she was a bit uncertain, she appeared in vaudeville and performed in several short plays. One San Francisco critic asked rhetorically, "Can this woman of almost 70 still act? Oh, yes she can—magnificently, splendidly...."

In 1918 Bernhardt bid her final farewell to San Francisco as an unofficial Ambassadress to America. She once again played vaudeville, despite the loss of a leg, acting in scenes where it was not necessary to move about. The news media claimed at 74 she was "as full of years as she was youth," and "as indomitable as the undying heart of France."

Sarah Bernhardt died in 1923, and the world mourned. The legendary Sarah was gone. It has been estimated that during her lifetime she earned over nine million dollars, yet she died almost penniless.

*Sarah Bernhardt as
"Frou-Frou."*

◆ ──────────────────────── ◆

Sarah Bernhardt in
Racine's classic, "Phedre,"
one of her finest roles.

*The enchanting
Sarah Bernhardt*

Courtesy California State Library

Miss Maude Adams

✦ ──────── ✦

Chapter 3

MAUDE ADAMS
✦ ──────────────────────── ✦
A Delicate, Elfin Actress

W ith girl-like sincerity, Miss Adams could put more acting and emotion into one scene than most ordinary actresses knew how to use during an entire play. She charmed her audiences as a mischievous Peter Pan, and thrilled them in "L'Aiglon" as The Duke of Reichstadt. Although Maude Adams preferred tragedy, it was the lighter side of drama that made her famous.

Maude Adams (Kiskadden) was born in Salt Lake City, Utah, on November 11, 1872. Her mother, Annie Adams, was a well-known actress of the day and a leading lady with a Salt Lake City stock company. Maude's father was John Kiskadden, his occupation unknown.

Maude made her first appearance before the footlights at the age of nine months in a play titled "The Lost Baby." The child scheduled for the part became temperamental in the first act, so the stage-manager seized Maude from her nurse's arms and carried her onto the stage. Maude was so cute and happy that she captured the audience and was an immediate success.

While Maude was still a small girl, her mother accepted a role with the Alcazar Stock Company in San Francisco, California, and the family moved to the West Coast where Maude spent her childhood. She began to follow in her mother's footsteps and appeared in several children's roles that were so delightful audiences started taking notice of the little artist. She was quite capable; and once a part was read out loud, she had no trouble remembering it.

Maude found the theater to be an exciting game of make-believe and took a special pleasure in applying her own makeup.

She liked to be consulted about business arrangements and, at the age of six, turned down an engagement because the salary was too low. Although she was still a child, Maude Adams was already a professional actress and was used to being treated as an adult. When it came to business, she was not an ordinary little girl and had absolutely nothing in common with other children.

But Maude was not all business, she had a great love of nature. In her autobiography, "The One I Knew Least of All," published in Ladies Home Journal, in March 1926, Maude wrote of visiting her grandmother and returning home to her father. She spoke of her grandmother's ranch with cows, sheep, horses, and dogs and of a young uncle who shared her adventures. She enjoyed climbing trees, roaming the fields, and smelling the sweet hay in the barn. The ranch could have been in Salt Lake City, its exact location is now unknown. Maude described a train ride and recalled the excitement of a journey across the prairies. It is possible her gentle personality and simplicity were developed and nurtured on this ranch she loved so well.

School was a problem for Maude as she preferred older people and found children to be a nuisance. Her experiences in the theater had taught her far more than she could have learned in a classroom, and her acting career kept her busy. After careful consideration, the family decided to keep Maude out of school until she was older. This made the girl extremely happy, and she was soon offered a new part in a traveling stock company on its way from San Francisco to New York City. Her father did not approve of a move so far away, but her mother found the idea irresistible, so Maude and Annie Kiskadden left for the East.

In New York City, Maude was bewildered by the temperamental, overbearing actresses and realized the importance of being generous and considerate of others. She also decided that it was the tragic roles she wanted to play, not comedy.

Maude's father passed away a few years later, and both mother and daughter returned to the California stage. Their world had changed, and life would never be the same. Maude missed her father, and things became serious; Miss Adams was no longer considered to be a child actress. She was apprenticed to a traveling company touring the small communities of California. During that period in her life, Maude learned it took more than desire to become a dramatic actress. She even considered doing comedy.

Maude's mother never lost faith in her daughter's talent and decided the girl needed more voice, dance, and rhythm training. As Maude struggled to learn these lessons necessary to become a good actress, she grew into a shy, self-conscious, unassuming young woman.

When Maude was 15 in 1887, she performed for a year at the Alcazar, then joined Frohman's Traveling Stock Company. Her previous training in stock companies, where she had played a variety of roles, had laid the foundation for her subsequent career.

Maude appeared in a leading role in "The Midnight Bell," under the direction of Frohman, and was an instant success. At this time in her life, Maude began to realize that comedy was a serious business; and she was ready to accept the lighter side of drama.

Following her success with Frohman, Miss Adams became a member of the Empire Theatre Company in New York City, where her performances were triumphant. Although she loved San Francisco, and the East was far away, New York offered continuous employment. In the West, it seemed, the supply of good entertainers far exceeded their demand.

Maude Adams was a slight young woman with large blue eyes, ashen brown hair, and a bewitching elfish face. She was a dainty person with a winsome smile and vivacious personality. Her kindness, lack of jealousy, and professionalism on stage earned her the respect and admiration of other performers.

As Maude's talent became more polished, she was offered the supporting role to the famous actor John Drew in "The Masked Ball." Under Drew's tutelage Maude learned the art of drama and sophisticated comedy. She remained with his company for six years, and in 1898 Maude Adams played her first great role as Lady Babbie in Sir James Barrie's "Little Minister." The comedy was done in Scottish dialect, and it was necessarily one of the most explained plays of its time. As a curtain-raiser, the mischievous

Miss Adams did a little sketch "Op'o Me Thumb," which set the mood for the play.

There was a certain glamour about "Little Minister," as all the Barrie plays were filled with the wit and charm of their author. Maude filled the comedy with life as she carried the audience with her, changing from minute to minute with both facial and vocal expressions. In this play she also offered her first tipsy scene which was considered deliciously funny and not a bit vulgar. The play ran more than 300 consecutive performances.

The next year Maude attempted to do "Juliet" and played the part with delicacy and charm in her own delightful way. Although she was sincere and genuine, the play received bad reviews. The audiences preferred the traditional dramatic Shakespeare to a radical departure from the usual form.

In 1890 Miss Adams appeared in Rostand's "L'Aiglon," the story of Napoleon II. Edmond Rostand was a famous French playwright, widely recognized for his skill and imagination, whose most famous play was "Cyrano de Bergerac." In "L'Aiglon," Maude played the role of the Duke of Reichstadt, son of Napoleon I and Marie Louise of Austria. The duke was a delicate, slender young man who died at the age of 21. It was as though the part were created for Miss Adams, whose slight figure and magnetic personality lit up the entire play.

From "L'Aiglon" Maude returned to Barrie's plays. Barrie was one of the most popular writers of the day, and his "Peter Pan" was one of the best loved dramas of all time. In 1905 Miss Adams starred in the role of Peter Pan; and her charming, elfish performances were delightful. During the play's three years on Broadway, she became the idol of thousands; it was considered her most famous role. Maude Adams revived the successful play in 1915, and later "Peter Pan" went on to become a movie. The first actress to play the role on the screen was Betty Bronson. In 1953 Walt Disney made the well-known story into a full-length animated cartoon.

During the early 1900s many actresses suffered nervous breakdowns. The intense portrayal of a morbid or sinful character for months or years created a mental attitude that strained their nervous systems. Maude Adams, although she did not play either type of role, did have a breakdown from overwork. Theatrical people who were acquainted with the talent of "Little Adams," as she was fondly called among her peers, said she was one of the hardest working and most conscientious women of the stage. In many of her plays, she remained on stage for the entire performance. In "L'Aiglon" her male role would have proved a tremendous strain for a woman of much greater strength than Miss Adams, yet she played the part for an entire season. Maude's lively personality and spontaneity needed to be refreshed, so she took a year's holiday.

Miss Adams returned to the stage in "The Pretty Sister of Jose" opposite handsome matinee idol Henry Ainly from London, England, and continued acting in San Francisco theaters. Two of her most interesting performances occurred at the Hearst Greek theater of the University of California, Berkeley. In 1907 she appeared there in "L'Aiglon" and in 1910 in "As You Like It." Her repertoire of plays included most of Barrie's works and Rostand's "L'Aiglon" and "Chanticleer." Her career lasted until 1923 when she retired from the stage at age 51. Maude's private life had always been quiet and serene; her home, where she lived with her mother, was a peaceful retreat.

Miss Adams was loved for the qualities of her heart and mind. Her performances were remarkable. She needed less publicity and advertising than almost any other actress of the theatrical profession and became famous entirely upon her own talent and charm. At the time of her retirement, it was said, "We have no other actress who can take her place in the theater."

Following her retirement from the stage, Miss Adams taught drama at Stephens College in Columbia, Missouri. She remained at the college until 1943, when her health began to fail. In 1953 Maude Adams died from a heart attack at the age of 81. She was buried in the private cemetery at the Cenacle Convent at Ronkonkoma, Long Island.

Miss Maude Adams playing the Pan Pipes in
John Barrie's best loved play, "Peter Pan."
She played the leading role for three years on Broadway.

*Miss Maude Adams as a mischievous Peter Pan.
This was considered to be her most famous
role and made her the idol of thousands.*

*Miss Maude Adams in
the leading role of Rostand's
famous play "L'Aiglon."*

MAUDE ADAMS AND THE MUFF

For hundreds of years people have been carrying muffs for various reasons. They were used to keep the hands warm or as a reticule in which to carry small items. Miss Ethel Barrymore, however, took the muff one step further in the early 1900s when she appeared in the play "Captain Jinks" and made the muff ornamental.

The San Francisco Chronicle, December 1902, published a column titled "How Ethel Barrymore Rediscovered the Muff." The following is excerpted from that column:

...If it was Miss Barrymore who made the muff ornamental, it was Miss Maude Adams who made it big. In J. M. Barrie's odd comedy of "Quality Street," Miss Adams carried a muff of snowy lamb's wool so huge that it reached from her waist down to her knees. Women were delighted with this muff. They said: "It not only keeps her hands warm, but all the lower part of her body as well. It is very picturesque to carry a muff so enormous."

And they went immediately to their furriers and bought, grumbling, the biggest muffs they could get. But these were not half big enough. Many, therefore, had vast ones made to their order, and the furriers, seeing, from the grumbling, how the land lay, fitted themselves out with a line of muffs much huger than those they had been carrying. In this manner the fashion of the big muff grew.

Miss Adams thinks the big muffs are delightful. "Yes, it is true," she said, "that I made them the fashion. That is why I like them so much. Have you ever planted a seed and had a fine tree grow from it? If you have, your affection for your tree is unspeakably great—the rest of the world can't understand it. Well, I have that kind of an affection for the big muff, and may its shadow never grow less."

Year by year the muff is becoming larger. Perhaps, in time, it will become as extravagant as it was 250 years ago. Men, as well as women, carried muffs 250 years ago. These muffs were so huge that parcels—dancing shoes, lapdogs and such like trifles—were stowed inside them.

The French have the words "Chien manchon"—muff dog. This word grew out of the habit of carrying dogs in muffs. Consult any old dictionary, and you will find the word "muff dog"—a little dog for carriage in the muff—for, in England too, this odd habit prevailed. Even in Italy, in the seventeenth century, the muffs of women often became temporary dog houses, and there is in Italian, as well as in French and English, a word for the muff dog.

Men's muffs were sometimes called muftees. In the time of Louis XIV, the bourgeois was restricted by law to a plain muff of black cloth, but the courtier's muff was a great, splendid fluff of gold lace and embroidered ribbon. In America young women made muffs for sweethearts, as they now make tobacco pouches, and young men were often embarrassed by these gifts. Franklin, in one of his early letters, says: "I have received of Jane S. a great muftee of red camlet cloth, embroidered with yellow flowers. It vexes me to carry it, and I am laughed at on all sides, but take it with me everywhere, lest Jane be displeased.".

San Francisco Chronicle- December 2, 1902..

Miss Maude Adams
in her later years.

Madame Helena Modjeska

Chapter 4

HELENA MODJESKA
The Polish Queen of Drama

Madame Modjeska was the greatest Shakespearean actress of her era. She was a woman of remarkable beauty who was famous throughout the world. For 20 years her lilting Polish accent charmed American audiences, while her love for her country earned their admiration.

Helena Modjeska was born in Cracow, Poland, in 1840. She was the daughter of Josephine Misel, a beautiful girl, who at the age of 17 left her humble origins behind to marry Simon Benda, a successful businessman. This union provided the wealth and position she desired. Following the birth of three sons, Benda died; and the young widow married Helena's father, Michael Opid, a high-spirited music teacher of impressive wealth and standing within the community. Opid passed away a few years later, leaving his properties to his wife. After several financial setbacks, the widow found herself faced with considerable economic hardships. She became close friends with Gustave Sinnmayer Modrzejewski, a man old enough to be Helena's father, who contributed to the support of the family.

Helena, at 17, was tall and slender with an ivory complexion, radiant dark eyes, and sparkling red-gold hair. She was an extremely beautiful young woman who did as she pleased and often disregarded the consequences. Many of the young men of Cracow sought Helena's favors, but it was said she only looked at one, Igo Nuefeld. Igo was madly in love with her; however, his pleas for marriage fell on deaf ears. He was of the Jewish faith, and although the Neufelds were one of the oldest and most respected families in Poland, Igo would never be accepted by Helena's Catholic family. The willful girl led the youth on, teasing him and occasionally letting him steal a kiss. Helena had shown great acting ability since the age of 15, and her only desire was to be the greatest actress Poland had ever known.

Mrs. Opid, however, feared Helena's flirtatious ways would destroy her chances for marriage to a man of wealth and position and had other plans for the headstrong girl. She had picked the well-to-do Gustave Sinnmayer Modrzejewski as her daughter's husband; and to ensure the success of this marriage, sent Helena to a Catholic convent to learn obedience and to complete her studies.

Madame Opid was content with this arrangement because men were not allowed in the convent, and the girls could not leave unattended. Helena spent a year studying under the watchful eyes of the sisters, occasionally taking a lonely walk along the flowered paths. This monotonous routine eventually became unbearable, and Helena's restless spirit missed the freedom of Cracow. Although she knew her family would be disappointed, Helena prepared to leave the convent. She first prayed to the Virgin Mary for forgiveness, then escaped over the wall.

Helena returned to Cracow on the eve of an ancient Polish celebration where great bonfires were lighted along the banks of the Vistula River, and young maidens wore wreaths in their hair as a symbol of virginity. As Helena joined the enthusiastic young people dancing in the streets, Igo appeared. It is believed that the impulsive young woman confessed her love for him, and for a brief time they lived together. Shortly thereafter, Helena returned to her home where she quietly married Gustave Modrzejewski. Some historians claim Helena was carrying Igo's child. Whatever the true story, Gustave was willing to forgive and forget; he was more than content to have an exciting young wife half his age. Igo carried his love for Helena in his heart for many years, and it was said that he eventually committed suicide in the Vistula River.

The newly married couple moved to Bochina, where Gustave had properties; and Helena studied drama until the birth of her son, Rudolph. Gustave had theatrical connections and was anxious to keep his new bride happy, so he arranged for Helena to make her theatrical debut. She appeared at a charity performance in "The White Camillia" and was enthusiastically received. Following that success, she and Gustave joined a group of strolling players, and Helena began performing in Shakespearean roles.

Tiring of the small audiences, Helena begged her husband to take her to Vienna, where she could perform in large theaters along with well-known entertainers. Gustave, though, was reluctant to let his wife stray. Helena was not content; and although the small-town newspapers raved about her beauty and talent, she wanted more. Madame Modrzejewski finally decided to take care of her own life and career; so with little Rudolph, she left for Cracow. Several months later Gustave died under what were believed to be mysterious circumstances. Helena did not inherit his properties.

Without the aid of her husband's wealth, the young widow was forced to return home to her family. She retained Gustave's name, and with Rudolph in her mother's care, Helena was free to pursue her career. She was quite successful in the Cracow theaters and threw herself into her acting. Times were hard during this period, with all Poland in turmoil. The Poles had revolted against tyrannical Russian rule and were defeated.

Helena was proud of being Polish and continued to appear in national plays. Wherever she went people defied the Russians by bursting into their national anthem and singing Polish songs. Helena's beauty and sincerity often disarmed the police, but many times she barely escaped arrest. When censorship became too strong, she turned to the plays of Shakespeare and Moliere.

One evening she met Count Bozenta Chlapowski, a Polish aristocrat and drama critic. Bozenta, who had spent a year in a Russian prison for revolutionary activities, admired Helena for her great talent as well as her patriotic activities. Since he was familiar with the stage, Bozenta soon became Helena's manager. With his money and connections, he took Helena on to Warsaw, where she became the leading actress at the Imperial Theatre. While there, she received the highest salary of any star and had the right to chose her own repertoire—something no other actress had ever achieved. She wore only the latest French fashions and became the envy of the prominent ladies.

In 1868, at the age of 28, Helena and Count Bozenta were married in a lavish ceremony at Cracow. She went on to conquer Paris and Vienna with her superb talent, then returned to Warsaw, where she appeared in over 250 Shakespearean roles as well as a variety of Polish plays.

Helena had many admirers and attracted both intellectual and artistic personalities. She and Bozenta entertained the leading citizens at gala parties. Although there were rumors of love affairs involving the beautiful Helena, nothing was ever proven. She loved attention and enjoyed being with talented people. If someone needed help with their career, Helena was always generous. Bozenta, unfortunately, was suspicious of her activities and accused her of having romantic involvements with others. Helena became increasingly weary of his incessant jealous rages and would escape to her villa in the mountains to rest. It was said she would often lie in her bed and cry for her lost lover, Igo.

As the strenuous demands of the theater and social life taxed her strength, Helena began to lose her vivacious personality. Bozenta's jealousy and the strain of so many intense performances were taking their toll, depressing Helena who suffered fits of melancholy. Her youthful appearance began to fade, and she started to lock herself in her bedroom, demanding solitude. Helena's only pleasure at this time was her son Rudolph, and her devotion to him increased as they walked together through the countryside.

Helena's friends were concerned and attempted to convince her to leave Poland. Bozenta was under Russian surveillance for supporting a nationalist newspaper, and a move was almost a necessity. A group of Polish emigrants had already left for the United States, and her dear friend Henryk Sienkiewicz encouraged the family to leave Poland for the freedom of America.

Helena finally consented to make the long journey and Henryk offered to go ahead to arrange their accommodations in the United States. Once the decision had been made, the dream of a new life was appealing to the weary actress; she started taking English lessons and began to regain her old sparkle.

While all of Poland wondered how they would survive without their genius of the stage, Helena, Rudolph, and Bozenta set sail for America. For her farewell appearance in Warsaw, Helena had played the balcony scene from "Romeo and Juliet." Following the performance, throngs of her countrymen had lined the streets showing their admiration and wishing her a safe return. Helena took this memory with her, and many tears for Poland and her people fell from her eyes into the turbulent sea.

The family arrived in New York City in 1877 when Helena was 37. They were amazed at the large city with its blending of nationalities, including Germans, Italians, Irishmen, Poles, Jews, and Scandinavians all living side by side in freedom. It was a refreshing change from the harsh rule in Poland.

Helena was offered a contract to appear in New York, but she graciously declined as she had not traveled to America to perform in plays. Her dream was a farm in California. The fact that she had never worked on the land before did not seem important. Bozenta, however, was clearly upset with his wife, knowing their funds, which were considered a fortune in Poland, would not last long in the United States.

When Helena and Bozenta arrived at the West Coast, they purchased an orange grove near Anaheim, California, and invited some of the Polish families to join them in farming the land. Unfortunately, the venture did not prosper. Bozenta was unhappy, and his fits of jealousy returned. It has been said that he vented his anger on Henryk Sienkiewicz and that Henryk left the struggling group. He went on to become a great playwright. Henryk Sienkiewicz's most famous plays were "Quo Vadis" and "Knights of the Cross." In 1905 he won the Nobel prize for literature.

The wasted talents of the great Modrzejewski were obvious to the theatrical people in California, and once more she was approached to appear on stage. This time the actress agreed. During her first "tryout" at the Grand Opera House in San Francisco, her accent interfered with her acting ability, and Helena left the theater humiliated. She was given a second chance by John McCullough, the manager of the California Theatre; and speaking in her native tongue, Helena overwhelmed the audience.

When she uttered the last phrase, there wasn't a dry eye in the house.

Helena signed a contract for a year at the theater, and McCullough anglicized her name to "Modjeska." She then went on to do a two-year tour of the United States and Canada. Count Bozenta was finally happy because his financial strain had been lessened, and Helena regained her sparkling personality.

She appeared in "Adrienne Lecourvreur" at the Fifth Avenue Theatre in New York City, and the critics raved about her performance. Her "Camille" was unforgettable. Helena portrayed the fallen Marguerite with a dignity and grace that no other actress had achieved. She was so successful the theater sold out for weeks in advance. Modjeska always had an accent; however, it only added to her charm.

Helena never lost her love for Poland. Many times the great actress would go to an ill-ventilated tenement to perform for her countrymen so they could hear their native tongue spoken in a famous play. She gave freely to those who were needy. Although she retained a deep devotion for her people, Helena and her family became citizens of the United States. This had become their country.

Helena Modjeska's acting was like a caress—she played her roles with a touch of innocence and winning appeal. In 1880 Madame Modjeska fulfilled a lifelong ambition when she appeared in England, at the Court Theatre, where she played Shakespeare on a London stage. She remained in England for two successful years.

Upon her return to America, Helena traveled throughout the United States playing opposite famous actors like Maurice Barrymore, Edwin Booth, and Otis Skinner. Her lilting laughter and wit were charming. Once, while at a dinner party, she was asked to recite a piece in Polish. Madame Modjeska obligingly took on a note of mystery and suspense and began to speak. Her silvery voice touched several emotions as she became by turns sad, melancholy, and happy. The guests fell under her spell; and when they asked the name of the play, Helena replied, "I merely recited the alphabet in Polish." She was also one of the few actresses of that period who dared to smoke in public. When someone appeared shocked, Helena would laugh and say: "You break bread with an Arab, and smoke with a Pole."

When she appeared in Nevada, the delightful actress played to a capacity audience at Piper's Opera House in Virginia City. While in the Sierra Nevada, the majesty of the mountains thrilled her so much that a waterfall was named in her honor. "Modjeska Falls" cascades into Fallen Leaf Lake in the Lake Tahoe Basin of California.

Helena Modjeska performed in Europe and the United States until 1905, when she gave her farewell appearance at the Metropolitan Opera House in New York City. On this special occasion, the leading actresses and actors all turned out to pay homage to the great Polish actress who had given so much to her profession and reached the hearts of Americans.

Helena and Bozenta made one last trip to Poland before retiring at Arden, their estate in the Santa Ana mountain range in Southern California. They continued to entertain, and Helena started painting and gardening. She loved her grandchildren and enjoyed having them visit. In 1907 Helena's health began to fail, and she and Bozenta moved to a small home on Bay Island, Newport, California. During that period Helena developed an enthusiastic belief that the cure for nervousness and neurological disorders was bathing in cold water several times a day. She would take cold baths constantly, claiming they provided a crisp, healthy appearance.

As Helena's health continued to decline, she began once more to have dark moods of depression. She would wear costumes from old plays and talk to invisible people from the past. Sometimes she could be heard reciting Shakespearean roles from scenes in "Twelfth Night," "Othello," "Macbeth," and "Hamlet." It has also been said she cried to Igo, her first love, for forgiveness and recalled events of her life.

In 1909, at the age of 69, the "Queen of the Dramatic Arts" passed away from Bright's disease. Bozenta and her son lovingly transported her remains to the country she loved, and Helena Modjeska was laid to rest at the Rakowiki Cemetery, in Cracow.

◆ ────────────────────────────── ◆

Madame Helena Modjeska

"The Queen of the Dramatic Arts."

◆ ———————————— ◆

*Helena Modjeska
in 1886 in the role of
Mary Stuart.*

◆　　　　　　　　　　　　　◆

Madame Helena Modjeska,
the great
Shakespearean actress.

◆━━━━━━━━━━━━━━━━━━━━━━━━━━◆

Helena Modjeska

*She so delighted audiences in the Sierra Nevada
that a waterfall was named in her honor.*

Adah Isaacs Menken

*She consistently shocked her Victorian public.
"Proper" women never wore trousers in the 1860s.*

Chapter 5

ADAH ISAACS MENKEN
The Victorian Rebel

Adah Isaacs Menken was known as the original "Pin-up Girl" and recognized as America's first burlesque queen. Wearing flesh-colored tights, Adah represented 112 pounds of daring femininity as she rode her wild Tartary horse up a precipice displaying an illusion of nudity that drove the audiences wild. Her toast to the Victorian public of the 1800s was, "Marry young and often." While she often shocked society with her free-wheeling antics, Adah never failed to delight the press.

Although there is a considerable amount of confusion about Adah Isaacs Menken's place of birth and background, it is believed she was born on June 15, 1835, in or near New Orleans, Louisiana. Adah changed her story so many times, her origins are obscure. She could have been Creole, Spanish or a Jewess. Her father's name appears to have been Theodore, his occupation unknown. He died when she was a small girl, and shortly thereafter her mother married a man of the Jewish faith. During her childhood Adah's schooling introduced her to the classics. She learned to speak Spanish, French, and Hebrew while growing up on the streets of New Orleans.

Her stepfather died when she was 17, leaving the family without financial means. In order to support herself, Adah turned to the stage. She made her first appearance as a dancer at an opera house in New Orleans. Adah was quite successful and decided to make the theater her career. After a year at the opera house, she joined a troupe of traveling entertainers on their way to perform in Cuba and Mexico. Following a brilliant engagement at a leading theater in Mexico City, Adah acquired the title of "The Queen of the Plaza." In 1856 the performers returned to the

United States to appear in Galveston, Texas. While there, Adah who was 21, met and married her first husband, Alexander Isaacs Menken, an orchestra conductor from a prominent Jewish family.

Her husband lost his fortune in 1857 and became dependent upon Adah for support. She eventually made him her manager and, as Adah Isaacs Menken, went on to appear at Shreveport, Lousiana, in "The Lady of Lyons." Her performances in that city, however, were considered moderate. Although Adah was attractive, with crisp, black curls and dark sparkling eyes, she lacked the bold, fascinating talent that was to appear later in her career. Her relationship with Menken, who by then had become a financial burden, became quite strained.

Following her debut in New York City, the couple decided upon a separation with the understanding that Menken would obtain the divorce. A few months later the impulsive Adah fell in love with John "Benicia Boy" Heenen, a well-known prizefighter who became her second husband. Their stormy marriage came to an abrupt end when the jealous Mr. Menken revealed he had never secured the divorce. The enraged Benicia Boy sailed for London to fight for the World's Heavyweight Championship, leaving Adah to face the scandal alone.

At this point in her life, Adah, who was pregnant with Heenen's child, endured her darkest moments. A baby boy was born only to die shortly after his birth. While Adah was still grieving the loss of her child, her mother also passed away. Benicia Boy's victorious return from England offered little consolation when he mocked Adah and denied they had ever been married.

Adah Menken turned to writing poems of despair. She occasionally performed on stage, but lacked the enthusiasm and self-confidence that were essential to good acting. During this time Adah met Robert Newell, recognized in the literary world as Orpheus C. Kerr, an author of satirical sketches. Orpheus, a gentle intellectual, was drawn not only to Adah's physical attractions, but to her sometimes awkward though sensitive poetry. She also met Ada Clare, a woman known for her free-wheeling Bohemian lifestyle and scorn for convention. Together, Clare and Newell helped ease the pain of Adah's broken heart and change the course of her life.

As Adah covered sheets of paper with her humiliation and spiritual agony, her new friends waited. When she wrote of the harsh treatment and injustices women in the 19th century suffered, the women's grief became her own. While men of the era laughed, Ada and Orpheus urged her to continue. They knew that out of these wild, often incoherent verses, Adah would emerge cleansed and ready to pursue the greatest acting career of her time—and she did. During this period Adah Menken and Ada Clare became close friends, determined to be free of the restraints society imposed upon women.

Clare left for a season in Paris, and Menken divorced Benicia Boy. Orpheus, who had constantly encouraged Adah's literary aspirations, became her third husband. With his help she began publishing her poems in newspapers and magazines and, in 1861, she returned to the stage.

Adah's new unrestrained acting and superb figure took the audiences by storm. Wearing a glamorous wardrobe, Adah returned to New Orleans where she appeared at the French Opera House. She then went on to play Milwaukee, Albany, and Chicago. It was in New York City, however, that Adah Isaacs Menken was introduced in the "Mazeppa," the play that brought her fame and notoriety. Her performances were greeted by expectant crowds, with every seat sold out, leaving standing room only. Tickets sold at premium prices to excited audiences that roared approval of the sensational Menken.

The popular play was taken from "The Wild Horse of Tartary," a melodrama called the "Mazeppa," derived from Lord Byron's poem. In this play Adah portrayed Casimir (who was also known as Mazeppa), a young Tartar who lusts after Olinska, the daughter of a Polish chatelain (keeper of the castle). The young girl had been promised to another, and in desperation Casimir (Mazeppa) mortally wounds his rival. Seeking revenge, her father condemns Mazeppa to be bound to a wild stallion's back and sent to his death as the animal dashes up a precipice.

Adah Menken, who was then 26, was considered incomparable

in the role of "Mazeppa." Her almost nude femininity shocked the audiences, as she allowed herself to be lashed to the back of the stallion wearing only flesh-colored tights and a wisp of loincloth. It was considered the most daring act ever performed by a woman, as both horse and rider had each to play their part to perfection. Adah was injured several times during performances.

Following her debut in the "Mazeppa," the popular actress and her husband Orpheus started quarreling. Adah found she could have her pick of men. Poets Walt Whitman and Henry Wadsworth Longfellow sat at her feet, while other males lined up at the stage door. Adah, however, often preferred the more prominent columnists who could, and did, write excellent reviews of her performances and love life. The lady obviously knew the value of good publicity.

In 1863 the now notorious Adah Isaacs Menken and her husband called a truce and sailed for San Francisco. Adah, who was to appear at Maguire's Opera House, was met at the dock by a screaming mob. Her arrival was followed by a great reception where the Menken so charmed the guests that the "Mazeppa" sold out for its entire engagement.

Maguire, not satisfied with the leading lady's already scanty attire, encouraged her to remove even more clothing for the benefit of the males in the audience. After a considerable increase in salary, Adah agreed to trade her flesh-colored tights for a simple blouse and a pair of shorts which revealed her legs high above the knee. This costume was considered absolutely scandalous and shocked the public to the extent that they fought for the privilege of seeing the "naked lady."

The news media were so excited they gave more attention to Adah and her horse than to the male stars. Subsequently, many of them complained of their treatment and threatened to walk out. It took Adah's charming personality and Maguire's generosity with food and drink to keep the disgruntled actors on the stage.

Adah was considered to be a daring, beautiful vision of earthy delight. She enjoyed every minute of it! Even when she appeared in other plays such as "The French Spy" and "Black-eyed Susan," Adah still packed the house. The fact that her costumes were always close-fitting helped to keep her admirers happy. It has been estimated that the proceeds from her San Francisco performances at Maguire's Opera House netted Menken the impressive amount of $9,000—a considerable fee for any entertainer of that era.

Praise of Menken's San Francisco performances sped across the Sierra, and the Comstock eagerly awaited the arrival of the enchanting actress. The *Daily Alta* announced her forthcoming visit to Maguire's Opera House in Virginia City, Nevada, by writing: "Adah Isaacs Menken will make her first appearance this evening and has chosen the character of 'Mazeppa' to debut in. That the house will be crowded to excess, there can be little doubt. She is supported by Messrs. Booth, Mayo, Miss Sophia Edwin, and the strength of the company."

In 1864 the *Gold Hill News* described Adah's arrival when they wrote:

> *She Has Come!—The Menken was aboard one of the Pioneer coaches which reached Gold Hill this morning, at half-past eleven o'clock. She is decidedly a pretty little woman, and judging her style we suppose she does not care how she rides—as she was on the front seat with her back turned to the horses. She will doubtless draw large houses in Virginia City, with her Mazeppa and French Spy in which she excels any living actress. On the occasion of her arrival Orpheus C. Kerr, occupied a decidedly lively and conspicuous position on top of the hind-boot. He was dressed in a black moustache, a plug hat, and a gray blanket, and looked like a troubadour or a Georgia major, just returned from the war. He also rode backwards, which particular fact confirms our previous opinions, to wit, namely: that there is something more than ordinarily contrary in these children of mirth, adventure, and bare-back equestrianism....Welcome to the Menken and Orpheus.*

Playbills appeared in the city describing Adah as: "Extremely beautiful, highly appealing, insanely confident and deliciously vulnerable." On opening night the theater was filled to capacity. Her performance brought the house down. They loved "The Menken." Mark Twain, who had previously condemned Adah, was lavish in his praise and so smitten by the shapely, vivacious actress that he never missed a performance. It was said he waited nightly by the stage door.

Adah was thrilled with the ceaseless, unending whirl of the Comstock's excitement. She spent many adventurous nights exploring Virginia City's hot-spots. The hurdy-gurdy shows, the bars, and the opportunity to participate in games of chance all delighted her. One night while she was visiting the Sazerac Saloon, Adah even "put on the gloves" with the superintendent of a mine. The man who considered himself a "bon vivant" was thrown within two rounds by the popular actress. While they were carrying the unfortunate gentleman out, Menken managed to take on two more of the boys, also knocking them to the floor. It would seem that during her marriage to Benicia Boy, Adah had gained more than a broken heart.

When the time came for Adah to leave Virginia City, they named a street after her, and "The Menken Shaft and Tunnel Company" was formed. The stock certificates were appropriately engraved with a naked siren strapped to the back of a stallion. The actress was so popular with the boys of the American Engine Company No. 2 that they presented her with a red belt bearing the company emblem and made her an honorary member. Upon her departure, Adah was given a $2,000 bullion bar in exchange for a promise to return.

Following her engagement in the Comstock, Adah divorced Orpheus and went on to even greater fame in England. She appeared at Astley's Theater in London, where her flesh-colored tights first aroused the anger of the Victorian audiences. Good advertising and Adah's own charming personality, however, managed to overcome social propriety. Within a few weeks Menken commanded the highest pay any actress had ever achieved.

While in Europe, Adah became a pen-pal of Charles Dickens, romanced Napoleon III, Prince Oscar of Sweden, and the King of Greece. She also met dramatist Alexandre Dumas, the Elder who, whether for publicity or love, shared his apartment with The Menken. Photos of the happy couple were circulated throughout London. Adah Menken was the first actress to recognize the value of photography for both publicity and posterity.

In 1866 Adah triumphantly returned to New York City and married her fourth husband, James Paul Barkley, a gentleman of considerable wealth. Their marriage, however, did not last; and once again the disillusioned Menken sailed to Europe. Her son Louis Barkley was born a few months later.

Following his birth, she returned to the Paris Stage where she played the "Mazeppa" and other roles requiring a scanty costume. For a brief period Adah became the toast of two continents. She attended parties given by the aristocracy, received costly jewelry, and rejected many romantic proposals. In 1867 Adah then 32, published a book of her own poems which became a best seller.

Unfortunately, success for Adah was not meant to last. Her excessive emotional appearances began to take their toll, and her popularity started to decline. Without the inner excitement and charismatic personality that were a part of her acting appeal, Adah's fickle public lost interest. She gave her last performance in 1868 and six weeks later collapsed. Her doctors were never sure of her illness, but it was believed she was suffering from tuberculosis.

On August 10, 1868, in Paris, France, Adah Isaacs Menken, at the young age of 33, quietly passed away. Although many have claimed Henry Wadsworth Longfellow was by her bedside, most historians believe she died alone. Adah was buried in the Jewish faith and first interred in the Stranger's burial ground at Pere Lachaise Cemetery. Later her remains were removed to the Jewish section of Montparnasse Cemetery near Paris, France.

Adah Isaacs Menken will always be remembered for her daring performances, enthusiasm, and constant battle for personal freedom in the Victorian era of the 1800s.

◆ ━━━━━━━━━━━━━━━━━ ◆

Adah Isaacs Menken in the "Mazeppa."
Lashed to the back of a stallion, it was the most daring act
ever performed by a woman in the 1860s.

THE LAST DAYS OF ADAH ISAACS MENKEN

New York March 20th — In one of our up-town picture galleries is a beautiful portrait, which is attracting considerable attention. It is Menken, the Amazonian actress. Looking at it the other day, it recalled an incident in her life that has never been told, and is worth relating.

One of the strangest characters the world had ever seen was Adah Isaacs Menken—a queer mixture of sensuality and mentality, she led a life, the peculiarities of which seem impossible to fathom. Her outward life is a matter of history, and it would be useless enumerating its chequered events. Her inner life she gave the world a glimpse of in the small volume of poems she published shortly before her death, some of them containing the most profound thought woven into the most poetic language. Living a life that was an open defiance of all moral law, sensual to the extreme in all her passions, she had a mind the most delicate and sensitive I ever met with—a strange being, she met with

A STRANGE FATE.

When she first went to England she set London ablaze with excitement. Thousands thronged Astley's every night to see her in "Mazeppa," and as many watched her day after day driving at the "Mall" with her team of ponies. Duchesses passed by unnoticed, even if they were young and beautiful, if "La Belle" Menken was in sight. Apparently impassive, casting glances at no one, with no companion except her "tiger" behind her, she swept over the Mall the observed of all observers. I had frequently watched her there, little thinking that I should soon know more of this strangely fascinating woman.

I was then a student at Guy's Hospital, and one evening the house surgeon—a gentleman who has since become familiar in his profession—said: "Let us go and see this

Menken the people are going crazy over. Have you seen Her?"

"No, except in the Park, where I have seen her driving."

"Rather a queer character I hear. But we'll go and study the lady anatomically, as she gives plenty of opportunity for it."

In a few moments we were rolling through the borough in a Hanson cab to Astley's, which is situated at the southern end of Westminster Bridge. Purchasing two stall tickets, we entered. In all of the European theaters, there are three or four rows of seats railed off next to the orchestra. These are called orchestra stalls and are considered the best seats in the house. The place was jammed, high and low, and it will hold a small city. The play commenced. There was but little excitement until Menken came on, when deafening applause rolled through the house. She was not very beautiful in face, but her figure was a model of

SYMMETRICAL BEAUTY.

We have all raved about the marvelous marble of Florence, that the sculptor seems to have imbued with life, but one glance at Adah Isaacs Menken, as she stood that night in her royal beauty, and you would say with Byron:

"I've seen lovelier woman ripe and real,
Than all the nonsense of their stone idea."

The play proceeded. It is needless to say how it was put on. It was perhaps one of the grandest theatrical spectacles ever seen, with a stage as large as the whole of one of our theatres. The steed fairly galloped over the mountains of Tartary, appearing and reappearing in the distance until the horse and the living form, bound on his back, appeared small in the perspective.

Suddenly a slight noise and a faint scream were heard.

There was a buzz throughout the house, the curtain was rung down. Then the manager stepped to the front and stated that Miss Menken had met with a slight accident—accidents are always slight under such circumstances. If there is a doctor in the house, would he come around. We were sitting close to the front. My chief said, "Follow me," and before you could say Jack Robinson we had scrambled through the orchestra and over the footlights to the stage. The manager led us to the green-room. There upon the floor, lay the beautiful Menken, her silk tights

STAINED WITH CRIMSON BLOOD.

"I don't think I am hurt much, Doctor," she said, "I'm only frightened." In turning a corner, the horse had gone too near one of the flats, and had grazed her limbs, tearing the flesh all down. Expedition was required. The room was cleared, and we were soon at work. The wound, which was not dangerous, but must have been extremely painful, was soon dressed, and the patient taken to her home at Brompton. The performance of "Mazeppa" was not concluded that night. The audience dispersed after having been informed of the nature of the injuries the lady had received. It was my duty day after day, to visit her; the wound soon healed, but the mental shock still remained. "I have been," she said, "for some years in constant dread of some accident of this kind, and the fright more than the hurt, has prostrated me; I shall never recover." We laughed at what we thought her idle fears, but they proved to be true. This girl, in the vigor of her womanhood, full of passionate life, with every sense strung to its highest tension—a magnificent animal, such as Du Marier loves to draw and Lawrence or Swineburne describe—began slowly but almost imperceptibly to fade away. For months she was carefully watched, then travel

was prescribed, and she went on the Continent. A few months later I received a telegram dated from Paris, "Come and see me before I die."

I lost but little time in reaching the gay capital, but it was too late. They say she died of consumption; she died from the nervous shock caused by the accident I have related. In her later days the power of her mind developed itself as her physical powers weakened. In her health and strength her mentality seemed to be overshadowed by her animalism. But, as the body decayed, the mind asserted itself, and she wrote those poems, some of which are as beautiful as anything in the English language. She was buried in Pere la Chaise; in a secluded corner of that beautiful city of the dead, near to the well-known monument of Abelard and Heloise, in an unpretending marble tomb, with her name, age and date of death upon it, and her epitaph, written by herself, in two words,

"THOU KNOWEST"

San Francisco Alta, April 15, 1878
Correspondent of the St. Louis Evening Post

Adah Isaacs Menken

*At the age of 31, she was called
"The World's Delight."*

*Adah Isaacs Menken
as "The French Spy," one
of her famous roles.*

*Adah Isaacs Menken
as she appeared at the famous French Opera House
in New Orleans, Louisiana.*

Lillie Langtry

Chapter 6

LILLIE LANGTRY

The Jersey Lily

She was deliciously naughty, exceptionally beautiful, and recognized as America's first superstar. Born on the Isle of Jersey, off the coast of England, in 1853, Emile Charlotte Le Breton grew from an enchanting hoyden into one of the most elegant and sought-after women of her era.

Early in her childhood Emile was given the nickname of Lillie; and as she reached maturity, it became obvious the charming young woman was destined for more than a life on the Isle of Jersey. Her exquisite cameo complexion, deep violet eyes, chestnut red hair, and voluptuous figure with its tiny waist were envied by the women and admired by men. Although she lacked sophistication, Lillie's genuine interest in others made her the center of every group.

At the age of 20, Lillie married the amiable Edward Langtry and sailed away from the Isle of Jersey on his yacht, the "Red Gauntlet." Unfortunately they were both disappointed with the union. Lillie thought Langtry was wealthy, and he felt she was a comely wench who would satisfy his every whim. The couple settled in London where Lillie spent her days reading and planning how to enter the whirl of London Society.

Although the Langtrys visited the theater and other public events, it was more than a year later before they were invited to attend their first formal afternoon tea. When the couple arrived at the gala affair, they found all the guests knew each other and were dressed in the latest fashions. Edward immediately became flustered, and Lillie, who was wearing a simple black dress with her auburn hair gracefully coiled at the nape of her neck, simply sat down and detached herself. She appeared so poised and aloof that she created a sensation. Lillie's loveliness and simple attire made her stand out from the over-dressed and bejeweled women.

John Everett Millais, the famous artist, invited her to pose for him; and Frank Miles, well-known for his pen-and-ink illustrations, sketched her classic beauty. Mrs. Langtry, it seemed, had been accepted into society! Her pictures soon appeared in all the shops, and invitations came pouring in. Lillie's own vivacious personality and clever wit made her welcome everywhere. Edward Langtry was bewildered by all the attention and eventually withdrew into the background where he sat in the corner like an old forgotten piece of furniture.

It was inevitable that the exciting Mrs. Langtry and Albert Edward VII, the Prince of Wales, would meet and have an intimate affair that rocked two continents. Prince Edward, who was usually circumspect in his romantic involvements, was so smitten with the curvaceous Mrs. Langtry that he let the world know how much she meant to him. Lillie was known as "the favorite" of the Prince of Wales. Whenever Albert Edward received an invitation, Lillie was also on the guest list. Mr. Langtry, who didn't dare protest, would pour another drink and pretend to look the other way.

Overnight Lillie became a professional beauty and the toast of London. Artists, poets, and playwrights admired her beauty, while the dressmakers fought over the privilege of creating her magnificent gowns. They allowed her unlimited credit just for the publicity, and Mrs. Langtry was dressed and groomed to perfection.

Lillie had always enjoyed physical activity. She was five-foot-seven (which was considered tall for that era), and worked to keep her beautiful, trim figure. In order to do this, Lillie would rise early every morning to take a run in the park and became known as the first woman jogger. When the Prince learned of her daily exercise, he began appearing on horseback to join her; and the rest of London society, though grumbling, soon fell in behind.

Most women of society were received at Buckingham Palace by Queen Victoria. It was considered proper and insured their continued popularity. Lillie, however, created a problem. All of

London knew of the Prince's affair with the charming Mrs. Langtry, and they eagerly awaited her meeting with the Queen. When she was finally presented at Court, Lillie defied convention. Instead of wearing the recommended small feathers in her hair, she wore large plumes. The presentation, although awkward, was a success; and the daring Mrs. Langtry again became the talk of London.

The Prince of Wales was known to be fickle and never maintained an affair for long, but his admiration for Lillie lasted throughout most of his life. He often changed his affections, yet continually returned to the fetching Mrs. Langtry. Her accumulation of jewelry from Albert Edward grew into one of the largest and most valuable jewelry collections in the world.

Their first estrangement occurred at a gala costume party, when the playful Mrs. Langtry put ice down the Prince's neck. He stalked out of the room because of the unacceptable display of intimacy, and Lillie fell from grace. Bill collectors knocked on her door, and Edward Langtry, unable to pay the debts, left the city in haste. The only friends to remain were the poets and artists who did not have the funds to help. During this depressing period, Lillie discovered she was pregnant and returned to the Isle of Jersey, where she gave birth to her daughter, Jeanne Marie. Mr. Langtry was not informed.

Lillie left Jeanne Marie with her mother and, with the help of her friend—playwright Oscar Wilde, went on to the stage. His encouragement helped her to succeed. Mr. Langtry became a defeated man who depended on a small allowance from his father and hoped only for a reconciliation with Lillie. He would not consider a divorce.

Meanwhile Lillie made her debut as Kate Hardcastle in a charity performance of "She Stoops to Conquer." Through this play Lillie's instinct for the stage became apparent. She was so triumphant that the Prince returned to her side, and never missed a performance. Lillie appeared at the "Haymarket" in London and was no longer considered an aristocrat. She had become an actress and, as such, a public person—something that didn't bother her one bit! Lillie went on to perform in Scotland and Paris, and every theater sold out to enthusiastic audiences. At the urging of Oscar Wilde, Lillie agreed to tour America.

In the United States, Mrs. Langtry became the toast of the country. Her notoriety and beauty, if not her talent, packed every house. While society women snubbed her, composers wrote songs about her. The most popular was "The Jersey Lily Waltz." Dressmakers begged to create her gowns at no charge. Whatever Lillie wore, American women copied. Tales of her love affair with the Prince of Wales and her incomparable beauty spread across the land. Demands to see the magnificent Mrs. Langtry were so great that many times seats for an opening performance were auctioned, and two dollar seats would usually sell for ten dollars.

Oscar Wilde introduced Lillie to the tall, broad-shouldered, extremely handsome and wealthy Freddie Gebhard, who instantly fell in love with the enchanting Mrs. Langtry. Within a few weeks the lovely Lillie and Freddie became an item. Only the fact that Lillie had a husband tucked away in England kept Freddie from marrying the glamorous actress.

Lillie had successfully toured the East and decided to visit the rest of the United States. Freddie felt that she should travel in style, so he gave her a "mansion on wheels." It was called the "Lalee" (which means flirt in East Indian). Along with the Lalee, Freddie presented her with a butler named Beverly who resembled an actor from an old English play. He was absolutely correct, possibly a little arrogant, definitely well-dressed, and absurdly out of place for a trip to the West.

Beverly presided over the elegant 75-foot-long home on wheels which boasted of a "Jersey Blue" car, adorned with raised wreaths of entwined golden lilies and a white curved dome. At either end there were teakwood platforms. The interior of this splendid car contained a drawing room with a piano and uphol-stered furniture, Lillie's bedroom (which was done in green silk brocade), two sitting rooms, two guest rooms, and a bathroom with fancy silver fittings. Beverly's compartments consisted of his pantry and the kitchen.

Wherever Lillie traveled, she became the center of attraction. The unwieldy car was so heavy it couldn't travel over small bridges, so Mrs. Langtry had to endure many detours. Newspapers carried stories of the amazing Lalee; and if Lillie had wanted to draw attention, she couldn't have picked a more fitting vehicle.

Although Freddie had purchased the opulent car, he found he couldn't travel in it. The moral majority of America was upset. Mrs. Langtry was a married woman; and traveling with a handsome man, who caught the eye of every female, was met with solid disapproval. Freddie agreed to meet Lillie along her route and often posed as her bodyguard. He was content to bask in the smiles of the beautiful actress, and his devotion was obvious.

While traveling through the West, Lillie made a special trip to Langtry, Texas, to meet the self-styled "hanging judge" Roy Bean, only to find he had passed away six months earlier. The judge had fallen in love with Mrs. Langtry's photos and posters. He changed the name of the town from Vinagaroon to Langtry and covered the walls of his "Jersey Lilly Saloon" with posters and press clippings of the dazzling actress.

Before she left, Lillie entertained the women of Langtry in the town post office; and with her customary grace and good humor, she insisted that the prostitutes be included. For the first time in Texas history, the "fallen" women had coffee with the "proper" ladies under one roof. Lillie was presented with Judge Roy Bean's pistol—the same one he used to keep order west of the Pecos.

The exciting Lillie not only thrilled the West, she charmed it. Freddie traveled with her to Virginia City, Nevada, where they were met by exuberant crowds who pelted the "Jersey Lily" with flowers. This was a special event for the local citizenry who had heard the many tales about the notorious, beautiful star. However, when Lillie prepared to walk from the International Hotel to Piper's Opera House for her evening performance, she claimed she couldn't possibly soil her dainty slippers and fancy gown on the rough, dirty street. She politely requested a carpet to walk upon. After a frantic search, the only carpet large enough happened to be red, and Lillie received what is believed to be the first "red carpet" treatment. From that evening on, all the famous stars demanded the red carpet be laid for them as it was for the Jersey Lily.

While in Carson City, Nevada, Lillie bought a gold mine.

Later, when she sold the mine, it helped to add to her great wealth. She went on to appear in San Francisco, Monterey, Los Angeles, and Yosemite. Everywhere she went, Lillie had mixed reviews. Her acting ability was usually met with criticism, while her beauty received raves. The *San Francisco Chronicle* wrote: "Mrs. Langtry has achieved something that is unique in the theatrical profession. It is not that she has made a fortune in four years. It is the fact that she has kept it."

Lillie loved the West. Its wild, untamed scenery excited her; and the warm, friendly people won her heart. She purchased a working ranch and winery in the Guenoc Valley of Lake County, California, and Freddie bought the adjoining property. Lillie's demanding career, however, left little time for the ranch. She and Freddie eventually sold their properties, and today her home is restored and recognized as a California State Historic Monument. Her vineyards have become a part of the Guenoc Winery. Although Mrs. Langtry spent very little time in Lake County, she always referred to it as "Paradise."

Following this tour, Lillie realized she was not an accomplished actress. She knew it was only her beauty and scandalous lifestyle that packed the theaters and decided to return to Europe where she could study acting without unnecessary publicity. Lillie entered the Conservatoire of Drama in Paris, France; and several months later left as a professional, self-confident actress.

Mrs. Langtry returned to New York City and was met by the usual crowds of people and reporters. When she appeared in a new play on Broadway and the final curtain fell, the audience went wild. The critics were enthusiastic and raved about her professionalism and style; Lillie was now sought after for her talent as well as her glamour and earned more money than she ever thought possible.

In 1887 Lillie, now age 34, returned to San Francisco, California, where she took out her citizenship papers. At that time she said: "I think it is an imperative duty for every foreigner who lives here to become a citizen of the United States." Ten years later, in 1897, she returned again to Lake County where she finally secured a divorce from Edward Langtry.

Mrs. Langtry and Freddie separated in 1890. Lillie went on to a new love, George Alexander Baird, one of the wealthiest men in Great Britain. Baird was an undisciplined rebel who had never worked and enjoyed prize fights and the company of prostitutes. He liked to drink, and on several occasions was known to have become quite violent.

Although the Prince of Wales and Lillie were still seeing each other, she developed a strange fascination for Baird, and the two were soon seen everywhere together. Within a few weeks they were involved in a torrid love affair. Baird gave Lillie lavish gifts, demanded all of her time, and often assaulted her physically. When she finally called the police and had him arrested, the story made headlines throughout the world. Upon his release from jail, the contrite Baird gave Lillie a new yacht, "The White Lady," which she graciously accepted. Lillie once more became the recipient of unpleasant gossip; however, she obviously felt the publicity was beneficial because she ignored it. Baird died a few months later as a result of a drinking spree, and Mrs. Langtry was left with a million dollar yacht.

While Lillie had numerous affairs and had always lived what many termed an "unacceptable" life, she shocked the world even more in 1899 when she married Sir Gerald de Bathe. De Bathe was a titled playboy and a member of one of the oldest and wealthiest families in Great Britain. He was also 19 years younger than Lillie. When his father found out about the wedding, he disinherited his son. Lillie, however, was not concerned; she had all the money she needed and cheerfully became the Lady de Bathe.

Lillie enjoyed her title and great wealth. She frequently visited the race track and started raising her own thoroughbreds. Mrs. Langtry also occasionally played in vaudeville; and in 1904, at the age of 51, Lillie again made the headlines when she appeared in "Mrs. Deering's Divorce." In this play, the Lady de Bathe removed her clothing down to a mere full-length slip, something no other turn-of-the-century actress of Lillie's stature would agree to do.

Mrs. Langtry, however, was more than a charming actress

who sought her own pleasures. She was generous to her family and needy friends in the theater. When Oscar Wilde was arrested for his unorthodox love affairs, Lillie remained his friend and helped to finance his return as a playwright. She provided financial support for Mr. Langtry throughout most of his life, and gave her daughter Jeanne Marie, her love and devotion, spending as much time as possible with the girl.

Although Lillie did not participate in the activities of suffragettes, she felt all women were entitled to their independence. During her life Lillie set an example by obtaining her own freedom; and though she was considered a lovely lady, she also proved to be a tough businesswoman. Lillie wore what she pleased, ignored the dictates of convention, and often set the fashion. She was a remarkable woman who adapted to life and lived it to the hilt. Always beautiful and vivacious, the Jersey Lily remained that way until the day she died in 1929, at the age of 76.

In this story Mrs. Langtry's name is spelled Lillie, which was her stage name, Lily, for the flower the Jersey Lily, and Lilly, the name of Judge Roy Bean's "Jersey Lilly Saloon." All three are correct.

◆━━━━━━━━━━━━━━━━━━━━━━◆

Lillie Langtry's life was so fascinating that it would be impossible to fully document her life in these few pages. In this chapter I have attempted to provide a brief profile of an exceptional woman. For further research it is recommended that one, or all, of the many fine biographies that chronicle her life be read.

— *The Author*

Lillie Langtry

America's first Superstar.

Mrs. Langtry
as Rosalind in
"As You Like It."

WITH THE PLAYERS
Lily Langtry the Chief Subject of Discussion
Society Will Make a Fortnights Pet of the Actress

Langtry is the topic just now. From the different points where she played during her progress across the continent, carefully prepared booms have preceded her to this city, until the last sharp, short shot was fired from Oakland, where she performed last evening. The interior papers have indulged odd vagaries in regard to the lady, preferring in some cases to criticize the actress from a physical aspect rather than to discuss her mental requirements. A Stockton paper, for instance, gives the measurements of the Lily's figure, including her limbs in detail, with the precision of a knight of the shears taking dimensions for a suit of tailor-made clothing, a luxury which ladies indulge in occasionally, to the disgust of dress-makers of their own sex.

It is of record too, that the heat wave, while she was in Sacramento, did not improve the temper of this favored child of fortune, and she rather snubbed the Sacramentans, who were a little tardy to welcome her at the theater. She did not consider what the lovers of art resident in the River City had to face: Two dollars per ticket and 115° in the shade. She must be an artiste, indeed, who could draw a full house under such circumstances.

Eastern writers are also busy with the name of the English actress. Although she has left the category of what are called the dude queens, and has risen from a professional beauty to a professional actress, the transmontane press are still descanting on her personal charms. Her beauty has so often been described, says one, that people who see her are generally disappointed. It consists mainly of a queenly carriage and a marvelous complexion, added to a certain charm of manner which would convince a blind man that she must be lovely. We find Langtry has become literary too, and it is said, has arrived at the conclusion that the pen, in her hands, may be mightier than the sock and buskin. Everything is possible to a woman with beauty and force of will. The serial novel she has arranged to write will be published simultaneously in English and American periodicals, and this will be followed by an autobiography, to be issued in book form and dedicated, by permission, to the Princess of Wales, A contemporary suggests, correctly, that if Mrs. Langtry should tell all she knows it would make a library, not a single volume.

San Francisco Call, June 26, 1887

NEW BILLS AT THE THEATER
*Mrs. Langtry Is Welcomed at the Columbia
in a Witty English Comedy*

Mrs. Langtry has not lost in the sixteen years since we saw her, her personal attraction. An opera glass fixed on her may possibly show some traces of the years, but the face is still handsome, the head has yet a beautiful poise, and altogether Mrs. Langtry is not in any material way less interesting than before. One cannot call her matronly yet. The natural graces of the society belle give her the old distinction, and she is very much more at ease with her acting than she used to be. She no longer has to ask for consideration for acting on account of being a stage beauty.

San Francisco Chronicle, Tuesday, January 1, 1904

◆————————————————————————◆

Lillie Langtry
1888

Lillie Langtry

She was the most celebrated courtesan of her era.

◆ ——————————————————— ◆

Lillie Langtry

*The famous artist, John Millais, declared
she was a Greek goddess.*

Miss Caroline Chapman

Chapter 7

CAROLINE CHAPMAN
"Our Caroline"

S he was known as "Merry Carrie" and had more friends and admirers than any actress of her era. Although she was not considered beautiful, Caroline Chapman's charm and acting ability won the hearts of America.

Caroline Chapman was born in 1818 in London, England. She was the youngest child of William Chapman and a member of a family of extraordinary actors and actresses. Various members of the Chapman family had played lead roles in London theaters for more than a century. Her father, William, performed at the Haymarket and Covent Gardens theatres in London from 1803 to 1827. Her mother had attended the Royal Academy of Music in London.

Financial difficulties in England brought the elder Chapman, his wife, and four of his children to America in 1827, where William Chapman and his son, also William, played two seasons at the Bowery Theatre in New York City. Two other sons, Samuel and George, married actresses; and the Chapmans formed their own theatrical troupe. Because of their remarkable and unusual talent, they were honored as one of America's most versatile theater families.

William Chapman decided to move the family to the western frontier, and in 1831 they initiated "Chapman's Floating Palace." It was one of the first showboats to appear on the Mississippi River and was designed to drift down the river to New Orleans. Caroline Chapman received her theatrical apprenticeship aboard this floating showhouse, where she played a variety of roles in comedy, mime, and drama. Miss Chapman was considered the most talented member of the family.

Caroline had a sparkling intelligence and vitality. She could play a role up or down and was a versatile, amiable actress and a quick study. Although she excelled in comedy and farce, her acting ran the gamut from classic tragedy to triviality. From the part of Lady Macbeth to hoyden roles, she performed with many of the great actors of that era. Caroline's style was original and free of the usual practiced stage acting. Her dramatic scenes would bring the house to its feet with thunderous applause.

Miss Chapman was slender, with plain features, a large mouth, radiant smile and expressive, dark eyes. She could put more meaning into a single glance than most other actresses of the day. During her appearances in the Western theaters, she was praised for her stately dignity and ability to play several characters in a single play. Caroline could go from comic singing to tragedy and utter abandon within the space of thirty minutes. She was always considered an admirable artist.

The elder Chapman died in 1843; and in 1846 Caroline and her brother William, who was affectionately known as "Uncle Billy," left the Mississippi River to perform in New York City. Uncle Billy was a comedian of considerable experience; and although he was much older than Caroline, he kept his youthful vigor. Their combined talents exceeded that of any of the other Chapmans.

The Gold Rush of 1848 attracted the adventurous family, and one by one the members started heading west. The first to arrive in Sacramento were George Chapman and his wife Mary. Their energy and eagerness to please charmed the audiences. The exuberant couple appeared in most of the smaller cities and mining camps. They offered their talents wherever a frontier theater, a small hall, or saloon was available. Their resourcefulness was outstanding, and they could rise to any emergency. From Sonora to Grass Valley to Columbia, the little mining towns of California loved and appreciated this couple. They were admired for themselves as well as their ability to entertain.

Caroline and Uncle Billy left New York City to join the family in 1852, and Miss Chapman, who was now a veteran actress of almost 20 years, made her debut at the Jenny Lind Theatre in San Francisco. She started in comedy and went through a series of role changes, becoming a popular performer in that city. She also appeared in Sacramento as well as the mining camps and towns of the Mother Lode and Comstock. Everywhere the modest Miss Chapman went, she was greeted by a boisterous crowd.

In 1853 Caroline joined her brother and under the direction of Junius Brutus Booth, Jr., performed at the San Francisco Theatre. She also played the female lead to Edwin Booth in his first attempt at "Hamlet." Edwin Booth was best known in later years for his roles in tragedy and Shakespeare. In order to further enhance her stage image, Caroline also appeared in burlesque, where her hilarious antics never failed to keep the audience roaring.

The San Francisco newspapers praised Miss Chapman's warmth and spontaneity in her roles, and audiences treated her as though she were their own creation. Her rapport with her public was one of mutual affection. Caroline had the ability to communicate; she was amiable at a time when actresses were known for their bad temperaments. It was said of Caroline that the lady was "beautiful and brilliant in talent."

In 1853, though, the lovable Miss Chapman almost fell off her pedestal when she and Uncle Billy appeared in a series of plays that ridiculed the notorious Lola Montez. Although the public laughed at Montez's eccentricity, they also admired her sensational "Spider Dance" and respected the many benefit performances she gave while in San Francisco. Lola, it would appear, was a poor recipient of low comedy.

In these nonsensical sketches, Caroline and Uncle Billy were merciless in their caricature of the popular actress. Billy played the lead in the "Spy Dear Dance," by grotesque prancing around the stage as a male danseuse, frantically attempting to shake the spiders off. Caroline mimicked Mlle. Lola Montez in an especially funny character named Mlle. "Mula."

At first the comedy delighted the audience as the couple poked fun at Lola Montez's acting and temperament. Miss Chapman had an outstanding gift for mimicry, and she was triumphant in her exaggerations of Lola's mannerisms. The play prospered for about two weeks when the newspapers decided they had had enough. The *Alta* appreciated the cleverness of the sketches and

Caroline's skills, but the play itself was described as being "Miserably arranged." *The San Francisco Herald* condemned it—terming the piece exceedingly course and vulgar. They felt an injustice had been done to Lola Montez who, whatever her faults, did not deserve such ridicule.

Lola Montez, however, didn't think the plays were all that serious and preferred to fight her own battles. Since her engagement in San Francisco was over, she simply ignored the play. The burlesque came to an end; and the newspapers settled down, apparently happy to have their "Merry Carrie" back providing the beauty they loved.

Caroline was never idle. She and Billy appeared in benefits and a variety of roles for several years. In 1854 Caroline supported Laura Keene as "Lady Rose Lawless" in a new play, and in 1856 she had a brilliant season in a comedy "The Actress of All Work," where she played several roles.

Uncle Billy was killed in a buggy accident in 1857, and his kindness and impromptu antics were missed by vaudeville fans throughout the West. Caroline went back to the New York stage a few years later. She did not do well and only appeared in a few plays. In 1861 Miss Chapman returned to San Francisco, where she played one of her major roles in "The Angel of Midnight." Following that engagement, Caroline acted only occasionally until 1870.

The new and younger actresses were hard to compete with, and Caroline, at 52 years old, had passed her prime. She retired in 1871 and lived quietly in San Francisco until her death in 1876. Lacking feminine beauty, Caroline Chapman's talent and amiable personality were unique among the actresses of her era. She was called "Our Caroline" by her admiring public; and like a glittering, expensive stone within a jewelry box containing bits of glass, she stands out unique among the entertainers of yesterday.

CHAPMAN'S FLOATING PALACE

The Louisiana Purchase in 1803 opened the 14,000 mile Mississippi River system to trade, and ushered in a new era of growth along the navigable waterway with America's westward migration. Later, colorful showboats started appearing along the muddy waters of the Mississippi, providing a valuable contribution to the history of entertainment and the theater.

By 1805 half a million enthusiastic Americans had moved West and clustered in small communities along the Ohio and Mississippi Rivers. The rivers continued to draw an ambitious stream of settlers and pioneers, and by 1825 millions of people had moved west. They cleared the land, built homes, established businesses and started families. The surging, powerful Mississippi River brought life and provided a means to carry supplies. Man was dependent upon the river for both necessities and transportation.

As the small settlements grew into permanent communities and cities, the inhabitants began to seek culture and amusement. The earliest performers were usually a vocalist accompanied by a tune played on a whiskey jug, fiddle, or harmonica. Even the crudest forms of diversion, such as wrestlers or acrobats, were welcome sights.

In the mid-1820s the first showboat embarked upon the mighty Mississippi. It was a flatboat, 25-feet long, steered by oars and poles. The first entertainers to appear upon it were a hardy group who were dedicated to their profession. Life for them was not easy. They were usually cold and hungry, and, as a rule, the sleeping arrangements were in a crowded tent on the banks of the river or wrapped in a blanket on the ground.

One of the first showboats to arrive was owned by Noah Ludlow and The American Commonwealth Company. The

performers, including ladies, traveled on a keelboat (a shallow freight boat having a keel, but no sails) nearly 100-feet long called Noah's Ark. The eager audiences would gather along the banks of the river, anxious to pay the price for entertainment. There was no shortage of performers, since almost every actor wanted to play the West.

In 1827 William Chapman, his wife, and four children left London, England, to settle in America. The Chapman family was well-known in the theater and had played leading roles in England for over 100 years. William appeared for two years at the Bowery Theater in New York City before deciding to join the performers traveling the Mississippi River. Every member of his unusual family was extremely talented, and all enjoyed their profession.

The Chapmans, hoping to stay together, headed west working their way towards the Mississippi. As they traveled, William Chapman played Shakespeare in theaters along the way, and in 1831 the family launched their first riverboat. It was called "Chapman's Floating Palace," a flatboat that supported a clumsy theater resembling a garage and designed to drift down the Mississippi to New Orleans. William Chapman planned to follow the river, stopping for one night performances at each landing.

Chapman's Floating Palace was crudely constructed. It was 100-feet long and 16-feet wide, with a colorful flag attached that read "THEATRE." The inside was divided into a narrow stage with a pit in the center for the audience. Hard wooden benches ran the width of the boat, and a muslin curtain and tallow candles were part of the stage.

The Chapmans quickly adapted to the river and from 1831 to 1836 visited exciting cities such as Natchez, St. Louis, and New Orleans. They needed no advance adver-

tising; word of their arrival was carried throughout the communities by other travelers. The whole family participated in the work and preparation for the performances. They were a fun-loving group who didn't have a schedule—and enjoyed living more than wealth. They charged 50 cents admission for the entertainment in the smaller communities, but would accept potatoes, fruit, a side of bacon, or whatever the audience had to offer.

In the larger cities the Chapmans performed Shakespeare and other plays as well as musical numbers, and the price of admission was considerably higher. In 1836 William Chapman purchased a small, fully-equipped steamboat known as "The Steamboat Theatre." It offered a larger stage and a new curtain with a painting of a girl dipping her bare ankle into a spring of water. The shocking picture of a woman's naked ankle, however, was too daring for the 1830s, so the scene had to be painted over.

It was this rich, warm heritage and family tradition that made Caroline Chapman so versatile and friendly. She appeared aboard the family showboat and in remote areas during her teen years. At an early age Caroline learned to delight the common people. That knowledge lasted throughout her years on the stage.

William Chapman passed away on board his floating theatre in 1843. Mrs. Chapman operated the business until 1846, when she retired, as all the children had left to pursue their own careers.

William B. Chapman

He was affectionately known as "Uncle Billy."

Miss Caroline Chapman — We sincerely question if there ever was an actress more perfectly at home upon the stage than Miss Chapman. Everything that appertains to her part — no matter what it is — is always well performed, and in a way that leaves little room for improvement. It is not in the most lofty tragedy that she essays to try her powers, and we are aware that they are calculated for the highest excellence in that department of the drama. But in everything where versatility and tact can be displayed — where sprightly vivacity and laughing wit appear, where singing, dancing, acting are all required, she probably has no equal on the American boards. There is a laughing, good humor evinced on all proper occasions, which says, "I enjoy this, don't you?" in such a way that an audience cannot help but be pleased from mere sympathy. Everything of the light and airy kind she enters into with that ease and freedom which seems to say that she is living and not acting the character in which she appears. In these days of complimentary benefits, we wonder that none is tendered to her, for she has contributed far more to the pleasure of the theater goers, than have others whom, it has been thought, the citizens could not do enough for.

— San Francisco Alta, May 24, 1853

◆ ━━━━━━━━━━━━━━━━━━━━━━ ◆

Miss Laura Keene

Chapter 8

LAURA KEENE

Actress-Manager

Miss Keene was one of the most remarkable personalities of the early stage. She rose from a barmaid in a London pub to recognition as the first actress in America to manage a theater. During her lifetime, Laura Keene's dedication to the stage influenced many young thespians. The strange influence of the Booths, Edwin and John Wilkes, caused her name to be forever linked with that of Abraham Lincoln.

Many historians believe Laura Keene's real name was Mary Moss and that she was born in London, England, in 1820. However, there are some discrepancies regarding the actual year of her birth. Her mother was a housewife named Jane and her father was a builder. The family was modest and cultured, and Laura was a well-read, respectable girl. Her father died when Laura was a child, and she spent a considerable amount of time at her uncle's art studio. The studio was close to St. James Palace and Theatre, which would explain her love of Shakespearean plays and her intense interest in the stage.

Although Laura came from a refined family, she was employed in her late teens as a barmaid. Due to her lovely auburn hair, the young woman was known as "Red Laura". She was noted for her beauty and charm, with deep blue eyes, regular features, and an attractive, slight build.

In her early 20s Laura married John Taylor, an officer in the British army; during their brief time together, they had two daughters. Taylor set up a tavern of his own, but the business was a failure. In order to support his family, he committed a felony and was banished from the country, leaving his young wife penniless.

Following her husband's departure, Laura turned to the theater and was trained by her aunt to be an actress. In 1848 she made her stage debut in Richmond, England, and in 1851 she appeared at the Olympic Theatre. Her performances as Pauline in "The Lady of Lyons" made it her most famous and popular role. While playing at the Royal Lyceum Theatre, she was discovered by American theater manager James W. Wallack, who invited the charming young actress to join his company in New York. Laura immediately accepted the offer and left for the United States with her two daughters and her mother. Laura was the only source of income for the family.

Laura added a fresh new personality to the American stage when she made her first appearance to a crowded house in "The Will." The critics found her "highly pleasing," claiming she "possessed a graceful figure...a bright, sparkling eye, a classical face and a clear ringing voice—attractions to which the audience could not resist paying a tribute." Following this play, Laura Keene became a leading lady with Wallack's company, showing great promise in high comedy pieces.

In 1853 Laura made an unexpected departure from Wallack when she failed to appear shortly before the curtain was to rise. Her uncalled for lack of concern elicited a considerable amount of bitterness from Wallack. Laura later admitted it was "a foolish act of youthful independence." *The New York Times* called her rash behavior irresponsible and claimed Laura Keene was an unreliable actress. Public sentiment rose to such a height that Miss Keene felt it necessary to write a letter of apology to the New York public.

Laura meanwhile, had gone on to greater things. She left New York for Baltimore, Maryland, with a lodging house owner named John Lutz and became the first actress to manage a theater in America. Historians claim that Lutz was her business agent and lover and that it was his connections that established Laura Keene as manager.

Following months of preparation, the first curtain rose at the elegant Charles Street Theatre on December 19, 1854. The *Baltimore Sun* claimed: "The company now performing at this elegant theatre are worthy to style as a Star company. Miss Laura

Keene who is herself an actress of rare ability, has evinced great judgment in the selection of performers, and hence every play is placed upon the stage in the most effective manner..."

Unfortunately, all Laura's hard work didn't lead to success; other Baltimore theater managers did not approve of a woman manager. Following a series of "accidents," Miss Keene was forced to close her theater five months after it opened. She left for California in the company of Lutz, her two daughters, and mother, traveling across the Isthmus of Panama; the trip was financed by John Lutz.

After a tedious journey, the party arrived in San Francisco along with several other performers, tradesmen, adventurers, and ne'er-do-wells. Laura, who was used to polished cities, was amazed at the phenomenal growth of what appeared to be an overgrown village. The countless taverns, brothels, and glittering gambling houses were astonishing. There was, however, a theatrical community, and it was there Laura Keene belonged. She was a well-established actress, and her publicity had preceded her.

Within a few weeks Laura appeared at the Metropolitan, where she received a true "California welcome." Her first performances were a hit, but as the weeks went by, Miss Keene began receiving bad reviews and was considered a failure. Laura blamed her mediocre acting on young Edwin Booth, saying he had continually disturbed her during the play and at one time had even winked his eye.

Disappointed, Laura and Lutz left San Francisco for a tour of the mining towns and smaller cities like Sacramento and Stockton. These cities had already taken a lead in California's theaters. The City of Sacramento was California's second leading city and in 1849 had opened the Eagle Theatre, which was the first in the state. Laura Keene's beauty and ability were met at the Eagle with great appreciation, attracting large, fashionable crowds for every performance. It was said that she captured the hearts of Sacramento's citizenry. Laura left Sacramento in a "blaze of glory" and went on to appear in Stockton, where she was equally successful. News of her sensational performances in these communities reached San Francisco, and the city that once rebuffed Laura now wanted her back. She spent the next few months entertaining in these three cities where she spread her charm and considerable talent.

In September 1854, with the help of Lutz, Laura Keene, now 34, again became a manager, taking over the Union Theatre in San Francisco. She refurbished the house and began to appear as an actress as well as a manager. However, bad luck once more ruined Laura's dream. While she was directing, a chandelier "accidentally" fell from the ceiling, striking her in the face and severely slashing her nose. She was unable to return to the theater for several weeks, and the venture was a failure.

At this time many thespians were excited over what was called "Australian Fever." It seemed a new lucrative venture awaited across the sea, and many of Laura's friends were preparing to leave the United States for greener pastures on the other side of the world. Laura had lost her theater and had heard that her husband John Taylor might be among the convicts in that country. She made arrangements for the trip, and with John Lutz and Edwin Booth, Laura set sail aboard the Mary Ann Jones for Australia. Her theater was reopened a few days after she left as The People's Theatre, but it was not a success.

Edwin Booth, who was not yet 21, elicited excitement among the ladies on board the ship. All aspired to capture the popular young man's affections in hopes of becoming his leading lady, but Laura Keene had already been promised the coveted position.

Following their arrival in Australia, the entertainers opened at the Royal Victoria Theatre in Sydney, with Laura Keene as the featured performer. The reviews were excellent; it was an exciting season for Miss Keene who impressed the Australian audiences far more than the charming Mr. Booth. The troupe moved on to Melbourne where Laura again filled the theaters. The newspapers described her as "... most pleasing and attractive in manner and very successful." In Melbourne the entertainers fell upon bad luck when an abrupt depression struck the gold fields of Australia, and box office receipts dropped.

The lack of attendance at the theaters and Edwin Booth's

drinking provided Laura with an excuse to leave the troupe and set out on a tour of her own. She made several appearances throughout Australia and spent time looking for her husband. When she and Lutz did locate him, they found he had been imprisoned for life. The *New York Mirror* wrote: "Lo and behold! She suddenly came across a convict dragging a ball and chain in Australia, who was the husband and lover of her early days....Was ever a good, noble woman more instantaneously ensnared in a net more deadly!" The experience was so disturbing that Miss Keene rejoined her company in time to return to San Francisco. The Australian trip had been a failure, and the disappointed group landed back on the West Coast of the United States only to find a financial depression awaiting them there.

In San Francisco unemployment was monumental, businesses were bankrupt, and theaters were closing their doors. Laura moved to Sacramento to build up her depleted finances but found the economy there no better. She returned to San Francisco where she appeared at the American Theatre for half her usual wage.

Determined to achieve success, the entertainers worked hard, and Miss Keene again briefly became both stage manager and leading lady at the American Theatre. Due to Laura's efforts and reorganization, the theater began to show a good return. She provided plays the audiences wanted, and the *San Francisco Alta* commended her for her "remarkable cleverness in adapting and bringing out pieces such as suited the popular and fashionable place of amusement." Miss Keene was acting and directing, and doing both successfully.

During the next few months, Laura presented Shakespeare and other plays, including "Burlesque operas," which were becoming quite popular. She took her company on the road to do the circuit, playing Sacramento, Stockton, and Marysville, where the *Herald* described Laura's ability to "flash upon the audience with rocket-like brilliance and rule all hearts and fancies as would the wand of a sorceress."

A number of changes, however, were taking place in the theater. The State Legislature outlawed theatrical and other "noisy and barbarous entertainments" on the Sabbath. Managers were being arrested for violating the law, and although the audiences were enthusiastic, the reduced attendance made little profit for the entertainers. It was time for Laura Keene to bid farewell to California.

She returned to New York where her wanderings in the gold frontiers and Australia enhanced her popularity. Once again Miss Keene left what was regarded as a "woman's place" to become a manager and opened the former Metropolitan Theatre as Laura Keene's Varieties. It resembled a huge barn and was so cold and drafty that a French actress caught a cold and eventually died. The large cavernous theater had an awkward stage that was hard to work with, and other male theater managers and reporters considered Miss Keene to be an intruder. Her sets were slashed by vandals along with attempts to keep the lady-manager from succeeding.

All of these obstacles were so upsetting that Laura Keene became severely ill; the resulting publicity, though, proved beneficial. Women came forward in her support, and male chivalry toward the "lone lady" manager caused indignant gentlemen to rise up in Miss Keene's defense. With renewed enthusiasm, Laura remodeled the theater and opened with "Old Heads and Young Hearts," which played to a house that was "crowded to suffocation." Following the performance, the "pale manageress" received a hearty ovation from an enthusiastic audience and glowing revues of her opening. New York's first woman manager was finally recognized for her artistry as well as her business acumen.

Despite her success, in June 1856 Miss Keene lost her theater to a rival over a lease on the building. A committee of company members provided a benefit for their manager who faced financial difficulties. The newspapers, who at one time criticized the lady-manager, rose up in her behalf, asserting that she had "displayed rare talent and energy...and deserved a kind remembrance." The benefit raised $1,500 at the box office and numerous monetary donations, some as high as $3,000 were received. Miss Keene's appreciation address was greeted by loud applause, and her first season in New York came to a memorable end.

New York, however, had not seen the end of the indomitable

lady. In the fall of the same year, Miss Keene, with the help of Lutz, became the owner and manger of the elegant Laura Keene's Theatre, and the next years were the most successful of her career. She produced elaborate extravaganzas with poetic taste as well as hilarious comedies. Her energy was boundless as she designed scenery, directed, and presided over the theater with a strong hand. Although the company called her "The Duchess," Laura was known to be kind, loyal, and able to attract and keep fresh new talent. She often played leading feminine roles with taste and dignity. Miss Keene governed her little kingdom for seven consecutive years.

In 1857 Edwin Booth again entered Laura's life; it seemed the "Booth" influence was forever to be linked with the life of Laura Keene: first in California, then Australia, and again when Edwin Booth made his New York debut at Laura Keene's Theatre. At that time he had reached his full maturity, and his genuine talent earned him the title of a star performer.

Following several successful years, Laura's theater was forced to close its doors. The changing times, along with a poor choice of plays and bad reviews, had become too great a problem.She was tired of fighting the press and of her managerial chores. Miss Keene gave her farewell engagement in 1863, where, supported by her company, she revived her most famous roles. This, however, was not the end of Laura Keene's theatrical career. At the age of 43, she began a new tour as a traveling star, first appearing at the Academy of Music in Brooklyn where she became a returning favorite for years.

Miss Keene went on to a new engagement at The Ford Theatre in Washington, D.C., in the popular play of the day, "Our American Cousin." She was in the theater on that ill-fated evening of April 14, 1865, when President Abraham Lincoln was assassinated. On that night the *Washington Star* carried this special notice: "A new and Patriotic Song and Chorus has been written by Mr. H. B. Phillips, and will be sung this evening by the Entire Company to do honor to Lt. Gen. Grant and Pres. Lincoln and Lady, who visit the Theatre in compliment to Miss Laura Keene."

The President's party was late that evening, arriving during the first scene. Miss Keene immediately stopped the dialogue, while the audience rose in unison to applaud and the orchestra played "Hail to the Chief." Following the tribute to President Abraham Lincoln, the play continued until the third act. Miss Keene was standing in the wing, ready for her entrance, as the shot was heard and the screaming began. A voice cried out "Sic Semper Tyrannis" (Thus ever to tyrants), and an impassioned young man leapt from the box. His spurs caught in the folds of the American flag; and although he fell, breaking his leg, he managed to limp across the stage. As he passed Laura Keene, she recognized the face. It was that of John Wilkes Booth, Edwin Booth's brother!

Miss Keene quickly stepped to the footlights and addressed the shocked audience. "For God's sake, have presence of mind and keep your places and all will be well." Then she ran to the box where she ministered to the dying President. A reporter from the *North American Review* wrote: "I met her at the foot of the staircase leading from the box...her hair and dress were in disorder, and not only was her gown soaked in Lincoln's blood, but her hands, and even her cheeks where her fingers had strayed, were bedaubed with the sorry stains! But lately the central figure in a scene of comedy, she now appeared the incarnation of tragedy."

Miss Keene was scheduled in Cincinnati a few nights later, but did not appear. It was several weeks before she could perform, and then refused to do comedy. She later went on to New Orleans and other cities and, in 1869 she published the *Fine Arts*, an elaborate monthly magazine for refined readers. Miss Keene also gave lectures and appeared in a few plays until her health began to fail.

In 1873 at the age of 53, Miss Laura Keene died of consumption. During her life Miss Keene's vital force in the theater established the "long-run" for a special play, initiated the matinee as a regular feature, and proved that a woman could successfully manage and own theaters. She brought charm and dignity to the American stage and was a motivating force to aspiring actresses. Had she lived in the early 1900s, Laura Keene would have revolutionized the theatrical business of that era.

OPENING OF THE UNION THEATRE

This evening may be considered somewhat as an era in the history of the drama in San Francisco, in the opening of the Union Theatre under the management of one of the most accomplished actresses, as well as one of the most finished artists who have ever visited this country. In the higher walks of genteel comedy, Miss Laura Keene has no rival in this state, and in the Atlantic States we know of no lady who could successfully contest the palm with her. This may seem high praise, still it is just, and in confirmation of our opinion we appeal to the general verdict of all who have the pleasure of witnessing her performance in the range of characters in which she has appeared on the San Francisco Boards . . .

San Francisco Alta, June 29, 1854

Union Theatre – There was a crowded house at the opening of the Union Theatre last evening, so crowded that we could not obtain even a standing place, and therefore can say nothing about the play or players.

Owing to the entire stupidity of the ushers or those who have the control of those matters, a large number of persons who had engaged seats and private boxes several days ago, upon going to take them found them occupied by persons who refused to give them up and to whom they had been given by the ushers. We would like to advise Miss Keene if she desires to meet with the success which we certainly wish her and which we know she deserves, to engage a new set of door-tenders and box openers who have some idea of gentlemanly conduct, and to see that no such blunders shall be made again as were last evening.

California Daily Alta, July 1, 1854

Miss Laura Keene as Portia.

◆━━━━━━━━━━━━━━━━━━━━◆

*Miss Laura Keene
as "Portia."*

───── 136 ─────

LAURA KEENE.

✦ ─────────────────────── ✦

Laura Keene

Miss Keene was affectionately dubbed "The Duchess"
by her company.

◆ ──────────────────────────── ◆

Laura Keene as
Peg Woffington in
"Masks and Faces."

SELECTIVE NEWSPAPER QUOTES
ABOUT LAURA KEENE

She is an actress of unquestionable merit — the most pleasing and popular that has ever visited Baltimore. Aside from this, she is exquisitely beautiful, and sustains an unsullied reputation for all those qualities of virtue which adorn and dignify women.

—A letter from a Baltimore correspondent, The Alta California, April 3, 1853

Instead of going from Sacramento to San Francisco, at the close of her engagement in the former city, this accomplished lady, ever obliging and urbane, at the urgent request of a large number of our most influential citizens, consented to take the route via Stockton, giving one entertainment here.

—The Republican, June 7, 1854

Miss Keene we all know is an actress of great merit. In a certain line of legitimate business she is probably without a superior in this City. Happening by a blunder of fortune to become a manager instead of continuing to be an actress, she unexpectedly developed a genius for spectacle . . . She possesses taste. The fanciful things of the imagination become pleasant beneath her hands . . . In Europe there is in every country one Metropolitan Theatre that is predominant for its scenic and plastic effects. Miss Keene, by her tact, good judgment and taste, has secured this distinction for her handsome little place on Broadway.

—New York Times, 1861

Courtesy Buffalo Bill Historical Center

Miss Annie Oakley

✦ ─────────── ✦

ANNIE OAKLEY
"Little Sure Shot"

A nnie Oakley was one of the most distinguished entertainers in America. Her expert showmanship and reputation as a sharpshooter made her an international celebrity. Wearing a fringed skirt and broad-brimmed hat, she represented the romance of the Early West and captured the heart of the nation.

Phoebe Ann Moses was born on August 13, 1860 in a weatherbeaten log cabin in Darke County, Ohio. Her parents, Susan and Jacob, were humble Quakers who farmed the land. Phoebe was the fifth of seven children and spent her early years in the arms of a loving, but poverty-ridden family. She acquired the name of "Annie" from her sisters who didn't like the sound of Phoebe. Annie was always a nature lover, and while her sisters played with their rag-dolls, she spent her time exploring the woods near the cabin.

When Annie was five years old, her gentle father was killed in a snowstorm, leaving the already poor family destitute. Her mother had no means of support, so all of the children, except Annie, were scattered throughout the county. She was sent to an orphanage. There, the other children made fun of the shy little Quaker girl and delighted in calling her "Moses Poses," a name she learned to hate.

After spending two years at the orphanage, Annie was placed with a farming family who promised to give her a good home and provide an education. Instead, she was abused, beaten, and overworked. Life was so bad for the child that in later years she refused to mention the family's name. She suffered two years of cruelty and starvation before running away. When Annie left, she took many unpleasant memories with her and a need to be frugal;

she never wanted to be hungry again. Later in her life, when Annie lost 80 cents in a card game, the loss upset her so much she complained of it for weeks.

Annie was soon reunited with her mother, who had remarried and was living on a small farm. The next years became the happiest part of Annie's childhood. She found her father's old cap-and-ball rifle, and after learning to use it, she began hunting quail, grouse, squirrel, and rabbits, supplementing the family's meager food supply.

Annie presented a winsome picture as she roamed the woods, enjoying the freedom and solitude they offered. The girl became such a fine marksman the top hotels started buying her meat and fancy birds. Her aim was so accurate that she shot the game only through the head, leaving the body intact. Annie's skill with a rifle was as natural to her as breathing; her coordination of hand and eye was perfect. She loved hunting and the feel of a rifle beneath her arm.

By the time Annie was 15, she was visiting the local gun clubs. Shooting had become a popular sport, and people turned out to watch the exhibitions where the contestants often received prize money. Annie not only held her own with the participating males, she consistently beat them at what was considered to be their own game. She was so good that a friend arranged a contest between Annie and a professional marksman, Frank Butler. Butler was 25 and a celebrated sharpshooter who had been married once; needless to say, Annie beat him. At the end of the exciting match, the shocked man, who had never lost to a woman before, said: "I have never shot better in my life, but never did a person make more impossible shots than that little girl." Annie not only won the match, she won Frank Butler's heart as well. One year later, when Annie was 16, the two were married.

Annie was a charming young woman who was 5 feet tall and weighed 100 pounds. She had an hourglass figure, abundant chestnut hair, and mischievous blue eyes. Although she was not a part of the women's movement, Annie was definitely a liberated woman. She wore embroidered blouses and fringed skirts which reached her knees at a time when an exposed ankle was considered scandalous. Her long hair was not pinned up as was the custom of the day; it fell below her shoulders under a wide felt hat with a star on the upturned brim. Although she was a part of a "man's world," little Annie was modest and feminine. She commanded the respect of all who knew her and was very much the wife of Frank Butler.

Following their marriage, Annie changed her name to Oakley, and the Butlers began touring the country as "Butler and Annie." As they traveled the circuit, Frank taught his illiterate wife to read and write. He refined her marksmanship and ability to perform tricks as well as the art of appearing on stage. Annie was an adept pupil and was soon able to flip a playing card into the air and fill it with bullets before it reached the ground. This became known as an "Annie Oakley," or a complimentary ticket with holes punched in it. Frank would often hold the cards in his hand while Annie shot the hearts out of the center. She also learned to stand on a galloping horse and shoot the flames from a revolving wheel of candles.

In 1885, when Annie was 25, the shooting team of Butler and Annie joined "Buffalo Bill" Cody's Wild West Show, with Frank as her manager. By then Annie was a star attraction. She could perform cartwheels and hand springs and run 20 feet, vault over a table, pick up a gun, and shoot her targets. Her performances started with Annie on foot running into the ring, picking up her rifle, and shattering balls in the air. Then she would jump on her horse and ride around shooting at various targets. Her most breathtaking act was shooting at a target over her shoulder while using the reflection from a Bowie knife as a mirror. Most artists used a real mirror, but not Annie; she was a showman. During the 17 years Annie spent with Buffalo Bill, she missed only five performances. It was said she earned close to $1,000 a week and estimated that Cody netted around one million dollars a year. It was a lucrative arrangement.

To say Annie was popular would be an understatement; she was loved by all, yet she never sought the limelight. One of her special friends was the Sioux Indian Chief, Sitting Bull. He adopted Annie into his tribe, calling her "Mochin Wytony's

Cecilia," which meant "My Daughter, Little Sure Shot." This title became so well known that Annie was usually referred to as "Little Sure Shot." In return, Annie taught Chief Sitting Bull to write, and he presented her with his first autograph. Later, before he died, the Chief gave her the headdress and uniform he wore in his fight against Custer, something she cherished all of her life.

Although the Wild West Show traveled all over America, Annie maintained a home-like atmosphere. She may have slept in a tent, but Annie did not live as a gypsy. She had carpets on the floor, curtains at the windows, and paintings on the wall. Annie loved to sit in her favorite chair and embroider. At home, the soft-spoken Mrs. Butler was very domestic and always ready to entertain a guest. She was so used to living on the road that in later years, when she and Frank built their home, Annie did not want closets. She preferred to keep her belongings in a trunk as she had for so many years.

In 1887, at the age of 27, Annie went with the Wild West Show to Europe. There, "Little Sure Shot" captured the imagination of the royal heads of state and hobnobbed with the nobility. At first she was an amusing little oddity, but as her talent and charm spread, she gained the respect and admiration of an adoring audience. She did command performances for Queen Victoria during the Queen's Jubilee Year, with many of the royalty of England and Europe in attendance. The Prince of Wales, Albert Edward VII, presented Miss Oakley with a gold medal on which was inscribed: "You are the greatest shot I ever saw." Then he said to her, "America should be proud of you," to which Annie replied, "I am proud of America."

Annie did some of her best shooting in England, winning $9,000 in several matches. As the guest of the Prince of Wales, she was the first woman to shoot on the grounds of the London Gun Club. Annie was so outstanding that the Grand Duke Michael of Russia invited her to hunt with him, and Franz Joseph, Emperor of the Austro-Hungarian Empire, gave her a rare collection of bullets.

During her tour in Europe, Annie received many expensive gifts in appreciation of her talent. Queen Victoria presented her with an autographed portrait of herself, and Princess Alexandra gave Annie a book of autographs from famous people, something Annie respected — especially Mark Twain's message: "You can do everything that can be done in the shooting line and then some."

While in Vienna, Annie gave an exhibition for the benefit of orphans. When the Baroness Rothschild presented her with a bag of gold, Annie donated it back to the children. Soon Annie's popularity surpassed that of Buffalo Bill Cody, causing a rivalry to grow between Cody and Oakley that led to the Butlers leaving the show. They continued on their own through Germany and returned to the United States, where they joined Pawnee Bill's Frontier Exhibition.

Annie and Buffalo Bill eventually ended their dispute, and the Butlers returned to his show. Miss Oakley was back with the people she loved and who loved her. In 1889 the Wild West Show began an extended tour of Europe which was very successful.

In the fall of 1901, when Annie was 41, the train transporting the show had a head-on collision with another train. Annie's spine was seriously injured, and it was months before she could travel. When she fully recovered from the accident, Annie appeared as an actress on stage for the first time in a play, "The Western Girl." It was a thrilling melodrama, and Miss Oakley displayed a new talent that surprised her friends and audience. She gave a first-class performance in a charming, natural manner. After playing to crowded houses in New York for several months, Annie continued to play Western heroines for the next few years throughout the United States. She did not return to the Wild West Show.

When Annie left the stage, the Butlers gave lessons in shooting and provided exhibitions. During World War I, they offered their services to instruct and entertain the soldiers and spent 12 weeks visiting various camps. Both Frank and Annie carried their own equipment and paid for their own expenses. Annie's faithful dog "Dave" accompanied them on the trip. Dave would hold a piece of chalk between his teeth or an apple on his head for Annie to shoot at, delighting the military audiences.

In 1921, at the age of 61, Annie was in another accident near Daytona, Florida, and her hip was broken. She never walked again without the aid of a brace. Annie was so near death that she had her gold medals melted and sold, giving the money to a children's hospital. The Butlers moved back to Darke County, and as Annie grew older, money lost its importance. Since the Butlers had no children, they were always generous in their donations to children's foundations and orphanages. Annie never forgot her terrible childhood and the name "Moses Poses."

In 1926 Annie died from pernicious anemia at the age of 66. Frank died 18 days later, and they were buried in Block Cemetery near the place of her birth. Identical stones with their names upon them mark their graves with the simple words, "At Rest."

During Annie Oakley's lifetime, she broke records by shooting 943 out of 1,000 targets thrown in succession with a 22 rifle. She fired close to 1,200,000 shotgun shells in 30 years; and in her younger days, Annie had a 16-bore muzzle-loader which she loaded with her own shells and black powder, cutting the wads from cardboard. She traveled to 14 countries where she appeared before royalty and collected cups, medals, and jewelry that were either won or presented to her. Annie Oakley's collection is thought to be the greatest amassed by any entertainer.

MISS OAKLEY WAS NOT SUPERSTITIOUS

Tony Pastor's combination will again appear at the academy this evening. Of Miss Annie Oakley, a member of the company, Manager Frank Butler writes to the New York Sun: "As there is much talk and superstition about the number 13 and the day Friday, I hope I am not entrenching in giving the experience of Annie Oakley. Last January Miss Oakley went to Easton, Pa. to shoot a match against William Graham, the English champion. Arriving there the day before the match was to take place she stopped at a hotel and was assigned to room 13. She did not notice it until the next day, when her attention was called to it by one of the betting men who was stopping at the same hotel, who said he was very sorry, as he intended betting on her, but now he would have to bet against her, and there were many others who changed their minds on the same account. Miss Oakley, however, was determined to show there was nothing in it, and won the match. Three weeks later she went to Philadelphia to shoot the deciding match with Graham. On going to the hotel she asked the clerk to give her room 13 if possible. She was told there would be no trouble in her having it as it was seldom used. Again she roomed in 13 and again defeated Graham. Since that time she has shot matches on Friday, winning all. Fourteen months ago she bought a farm in Illinois, paying $4,000 for it. The sale was made on Friday. Three months ago a railroad ran close to it, and she has just sold it for $6,000. She has three matches to shoot this fall. They are all on Friday, and she says she wants room 13 each time. I might also mention the fact that she was born August 13th."

—The Post Express, Wednesday, 1888
From Annie Oakley's Scrapbook
Courtesy Buffalo Bill Historical Center, Cody, Wyoming

"Buffalo Bill" Cody

SKETCHES AT THE WILD WEST SHOW

Buffalo Bill returned to Earl's court, the scene of his former triumphs in London, after a long European tour and the prestige of hazardous services successfully rendered by him on the field of battle. Colonel Cody won his spurs, all the civilized world knows, as a trustworthy scout attached to the United States Army; and his presence on active duty during the Indian outbreak at Pine Ridge, Dakota, is of such recent occurrence as to need no further comment heard. An added interest to the present Wild West Show lies in the fact that Colonel Cody is accompanied by twenty military hostages, Indians engaged in the late rising (by permission of his Government). There are between sixty and seventy Indians altogether, braves, squaws, and children, who take part in the present exhibition.

The merits of the show rest solely upon its natural features, and not upon any artificial aids. The Indians are Indians in their warpaint and feathers, and the horses are the Mexican mustangs and "broncos" of the plains, while the horsemanship is so undeniably good that a succession of visits does not pall upon the spectator.

Our sketches severally illustrate some of the more remarkable incidents; for example, the mounting in hot haste of the Pony Express, showing the method by which letters and despatches of the republic were formerly carried across the vast American continent previous to the introduction of railways and telegraphs. Hunting the buffalo in the Far West, a scene of sufficient realism, considering these same buffaloes are hunted twice a day; it is even possible they may enjoy it as a rough and tumble game, seeing that they do not get killed. Lassoing horses is another interesting feature.

There was a dance of the Red Skins; Lone Wolf, a Sioux chief; a cowboy on a "bucking" horse, and Colonel Cody himself on his famous white horse, carrying his trusty rifle "Lucretia" across the pommel of his saddle, a characteristic habit of his when on duty in the field.

In addition to these, there is the remarkable shooting of Miss Annie Oakley, whose expertness with the rifle is phenomenal; an attack on an emigrant train by Indians, which is decidedly picturesque; the capture of the Deadwood mail coach and subsequent rescue by Buffalo Bill and his Cowboys, and some clever sharp-shooting by the redoubtable Colonel himself. It is an exciting programme, admirably carried out, and well managed by all concerned. The whole party are encamped in the grounds adjoining the arena, and the Indians and their painted tents provide a never failing source of interest to the visitors, who crowd the sidewalks of an afternoon after the exhibition is over.

—The Queen, The Lady's Newspaper
May 28, 1892
From Annie Oakley's Scrapbook
Courtesy Buffalo Bill Historical Center
Cody, Wyoming

*A poster advertising Miss Annie Oakley
in Buffalo Bill's Wild West show.*

KING OFFERS TO BUY ANNIE OAKLEY

An amusing incident it is said recently occurred in connection with this popular lady shootist. Dinale Sulifon, King of Senegal, visited the Wild West show, and was so impressed with Miss Oakley's shooting that he proposed purchasing her for 100,000 francs and taking her home to exterminate the wild beasts within his domain. His Majesty was greatly surprised when told he could by no right purchase her and she was not for sale, and knit his black brow. It was too good a joke to keep from "Little Sure Shot," and the proposition was submitted to her. It was said she archly replied that she felt highly honored but thought she should prefer shooting for the delectation of the dear public and her bread and Butler.

—New York Herald, 1889
From Annie Oakley's Scrapbook
Courtesy Buffalo Bill Historical Center
Cody, Wyoming

ANNIE OAKLEY DECLARED DEAD —
WHILE VERY MUCH ALIVE

Notes

The statement, which has been going the rounds of the press that Miss Annie Oakley had died of congestion of the lungs in Buenos Ayres, is not correct, as Miss Oakley is not dead, nor was she in Buenos Ayres. As mentioned in these columns a short time since, when Miss Oakley concluded her European Continental tour with Buffalo Bill, she settled in England for the Winter, and has been there ever since. Last Friday, when the papers were burying her, we received a letter from her husband, Mr. Frank B. Butler, stating they were visiting Mr. and Mrs. William Graham, at the Royal Oak Hotel, Ashford, England, where Miss Oakley was also shooting game. In the letter, Mr. Butler enclosed a clipping from the British Express and Ashford News mentioning Miss Oakley's presence at the Royal Oak Hotel Starling Shoot, and the wonderful shots she made with a pistol, invariably hitting the edge of a visiting card, held edgeways to her by Mr. Butler or Mr. Graham at a distance from ten to twenty paces; and with a Holland 3-20 double rifle, she hit successively two marbles thrown in the air, and with a repeating rifle she split with the first shot a piece of brick, as it was thrown up, and with the second shot knocked to pieces one of the fragments as it descended. She also struck half-penney and six pence pieces, thrown up in the same way. It will therefore be seen that Little Sure Shot was a very lively corpse in England, when she was supposed to be a very quiet one in Buenos Ayres; and we hope it will be a very long time before we have to write her obituary.

—The American Field, 1891
From Annie Oakley's Scrapbook
Courtesy Buffalo Bill Historical Center, Cody, Wyoming

A CARD FROM MISS ANNIE OAKLEY

Editor Shooting and Fishing: — I am, indeed very grateful for your many kind words in my obituary. How such a report started I do not know. I am thankful to say I am in the best of health. Like all bad news, it traveled fast, and caused me and mine no end of trouble. Indeed, while I am writing I have before me a letter from my sister, and this is the picture she draws: A mother, old and feeble, in a lonely farmhouse, more than four thousand miles from me, who for two days has sat and cried for the one she loved and thought dead and gone, and how glad she was when she received my cablegram, saying I am alive and well.

To the many kind friends, whose letters and telegrams I have been unable to answer, I extend my thanks, and I hope to again meet all old friends.

I hope you will publish this letter, or at least enough of it to let my friends know I am alive and well.

—Ashford, Kent, England, January 15, 1891
The American Stream, 1891
From Annie Oakley's Scrapbook
Courtesy Buffalo Bill Historical Center
Cody, Wyoming

Courtesy Buffalo Bill Historical Center

"*Little Sure Shot.*"

Courtesy Lake County Museum

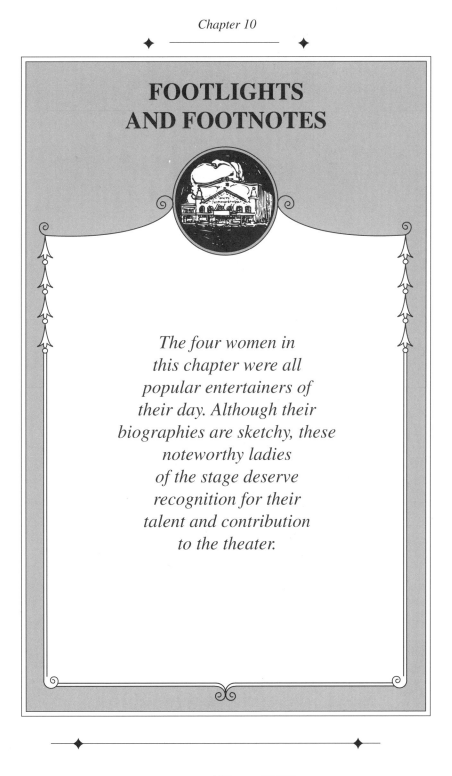

Chapter 10

FOOTLIGHTS
AND FOOTNOTES

*The four women in
this chapter were all
popular entertainers of
their day. Although their
biographies are sketchy, these
noteworthy ladies
of the stage deserve
recognition for their
talent and contribution
to the theater.*

◆————————————————————————◆

Florenz Tamara in
"Lollipop."

FLORENZ TAMARA

◆ ——————————————————— ◆

Florenz Tamara was a charming blonde toe dancer of Russian and Scandinavian descent who grew up on the West Coast of California. She was pretty, shapely, and very talented. It was said she could dance gracefully while wearing lingerie and not shock even the most modest person.

Miss Tamara appeared as a solo performer in several night-clubs and almost became the dancing partner of the famed Rudolph Valentino. She was dancing at the Techo Tavern in San Francisco when the young Italian walked in. He gazed at Miss Tamara with his "liquid" eyes and proposed that they form a dancing partnership.

Florenz was receiving a fine salary at the time and did not care to exchange it for something less. Valentino, however, was so persuasive that she decided to give it a try. When the couple started to dance, she found, to her surprise, that while Valentino had liquid eyes, he also had lead feet.

Two days later, before they were to open at the Alcazar, Miss Tamara asked what their salary was to be. When she found out it was a mere $75 a week, the talented lady returned to the tavern, declaring the wear and tear on her feet while dancing with the "Sheik" was worth five times that amount.

In 1922 Florenz Tamara met Addison Fowler, and they formed the dance team of Fowler and Tamara. The couple established a wide following throughout America and appeared at theaters with entertainers like Harold Lloyd, Will Rogers, Alan Hale, Buster Keaton, and Paul Ash and his Syno-Symphonists. The dancing team was hailed as "The Castles of the West." Their performance at the Majestic Dancing Pavilion in San Francisco was the biggest hit the dancing academy had ever witnessed.

Leaving San Francisco, Fowler and Tamara traveled the East, appearing in several notable productions, culminating their wonderful success as headliners in the "Ziegfeld Midnight Frolic." They were considered "Dance Artists Supreme," and their performances in New York became a sensation. The Jazzing Toe Trot, their own original dance, was a modernized version of the Russian Ballet. Miss Tamara was noted for her skill in an East Indian slave dance. At the end of the dance, she lay extended across the shoulders of Mr. Fowler and was whirled with such rapidity that the pair resembled a human top.

Fowler and Tamara played top vaudeville houses including the Palace in New York. They traveled abroad and did command performances for the royal families of Spain, Denmark, Portugal, and a Maharajah in India. While in Paris the American dancers starred at the Folies Bergere; and in Great Britain they gave a command performance for Edward, the Prince of Wales, and Princess Helena Victoria.

In 1924 the dancing duo were married backstage at the Knickerbocker Theatre in New York City following a performance of "Lollipop." The New York Morning Telegraph wrote: "Romance is a sprightly fellow...his is a merry life....He rubbed his hands together in high glee when he first saw Fowler and Tamara."

Later in 1924 special music was broadcast by radio at the Aeolian Hall in New York and used for the first time to accompany dancers in a public place before an audience. Florenz Tamara and Addison Fowler danced to the strains of "The One I Love Belongs to Someone Else" from WJZ Radio Corporation of America atop Aeolian Hall. As a large audience listened to the dance music, the announcer described the steps to the listeners.

While in the Midwest, Fowler and Tamara's distinctive dancing was so entertaining that everyone wanted to dance! The Wisconsin News ran a special daily column to teach the art of dancing. A new lesson appeared step by step every day.

Back in the West, Fowler and Tamara developed the Tamara Tango, which was danced on almost every dance floor from San Francisco to Seattle, and the Pony Trot, which was presented at the Exposition Auditorium in San Francisco. They also appeared at the Palais Royal and Grauman's in Los Angeles and performed so gracefully that one's eye was never turned away while they were in the spotlight.

During their career the dancing team of Fowler and Tamara was noted for their talented dance interpretations and gorgeous costumes. They were headliners of the first class and always had the star dressing room. When they retired from the stage in 1942, they managed the Arthur Murray Dance School in Providence, Rhode Island, and later established the Fowler and Tamara School of Dance.

◆————————————————————————◆

This story was obtained from numerous newspaper articles and reviews from Florenz Tamara's scrapbook, courtesy of the Lake County Museum. Miss Tamara passed away in 1946, her date of birth is unknown. Tamara's scrapbook and many of her elaborate costumes can be found at the museum.

Courtesy Lake County Museum

Addison Fowler
and
Florenz Tamara

When Fowler and Tamara, dancers who appeared at the Miller last week, reached Kansas City, they went to the baggage car to get Miss Tamara's beautiful St. Bernard dog which goes with them. There was nothing left except a collar and chain, and now Miss Tamara has written to learn if the dog is in Wichita. It is an animal of enormous size and shorn like a lion. It attracted attention while the dancers were here.

Wichita Eagle, August 1922

She Dares to Lend Atmosphere to Picture — The charm of Florenz Tamara is gracefully outlined in a Chinese costume this week at the Newman, where she, with her partner, Addison Fowler, are dancing in an atmospheric prologue to "East is West." The costumes of both the dancers are probably the most gorgeous ever seen here. And their ability as dancers is undeniable, lending Oriental setting to Constance Talmadge as Ming Toy in the film version of the famous stage play.

Kansas City Post, 1922

Courtesy Lake County Museum

Corabelle Knight

CORABELLE KNIGHT

◆————————————————————————————————————◆

The musically gifted Corabelle Knight was born in Canton, Ohio, in 1876. Her father, George Knight, was an American pioneer in the tire industry and played an important role in the development of the Willys-Knight automobile.

Corabelle was raised in a wealthy, cultured environment and learned to have a fine appreciation for music and the arts. She was a tall, slender, attractive young woman with expressive blue eyes, and thick reddish-brown hair, who took great pleasure in painting. Upon her graduation from finishing school, she was already an accomplished pianist. In order to further her education, Corabelle traveled to Europe where she attended the finest schools of music. In 1904, at the age of 28, Miss Knight met her future husband, George Piner, also a student of music.

Mr. Piner was the son of a local merchant in the small community of Kelseyville, California. He was a handsome man who had always enjoyed music and possessed a remarkable voice. Unlike Corabelle, George's early training was received by singing in a church choir and participating in local programs. He attended the local music academy before going to San Francisco and Europe where he could further his voice lessons.

Corabelle and George were married in London, England, and continued their education in Europe. In Varsovie, Poland, while the couple were studying under the great music teacher Edouard De' Reszke, it was discovered that Corabelle also had a beautiful voice. With De'Reszke's expert training, she became one of the world's most famous lyric sopranos. Her voice was considered to be in the same class with such artists as Melba, Schumann-Heink, and others of high merit. De'Reszke developed George Piner's voice into a fine tenor which rivaled that of the great Caruso.

The couple toured Europe, where they were in great demand.

They were billed as Signor Giorgio Pinero and Signorina Coria Bellini because most Europeans felt Americans lacked sophistication and polish. As "The Great Pinero" and "Coria Bellini," they entertained the European heads of state and received many exquisite gifts in appreciation of their outstanding talents. Coria was at times in greater demand in Europe than the famous pianist Paderewski. Wherever the Piners entertained, they collected beautiful art treasures, tapestries, and fine furnishings that later went into their Nob Hill home in San Francisco.

In 1909, when Corabelle was 33, the Piners returned to tour America. They appeared in New York, Philadelphia, Omaha, Denver, Sacramento, San Francisco and other cities. The 1910 *New York Independent* wrote: "Too much praise cannot be given Signorina Bellini whose splendid voice charmed everyone, as was plainly indicated by the recognition given every selection. Each number was received with warm applause and hearty encores."

In 1915 George Piner suffered an accident and could no longer stand on the concert stage, so he and Corabelle opened their own academy of music in San Francisco. They later bought a vacation residence in George's hometown of Kelseyville, where the couple would bring their students each summer. The Piners did not have any children; their students were their family.

In 1930, when Corabelle was 64, Kelseyville became the Piner's permanent home, they continued to teach music and have recitals until their health began to fail. Corabelle died in 1952, at the age of 76, and George died the following day. Their love for each other was so great that one could not live without the other. The Piners were buried side by side in the cemetery in Kelseyville.

The information for Corabelle Knight's story was obtained from Mrs. Ruby Glebe of Lakeport, California. Mrs. Glebe and her husband purchased the beautiful, ornate furniture and valuable treasures that were in the Piner residence. Corabelle's elegant wardrobe of voile, silks, and lace are on display at the Lake County Museum in Lakeport, California.

Courtesy Ruby Glebe

◆━━━━━━━━━━━━━━━━◆

Corabelle Knight
Pianist and Lyric Soprano

Blanche Bates
as "The Girl of the Golden West."

BLANCHE BATES

A lthough there is very little biographical background on Blanche Bates, she was a popular actress of the early 1900s who appeared in several well-known plays. Her parents were entertainers with a traveling stock company which played the Alabama circuit throughout the Civil War, before appearing in the West. They were performing in Portland, Oregon, in 1873 when Blanche was born.

Following her birth, Blanche's father took his wife and child to San Francisco. There he managed a theater with her mother as the leading lady. He eventually opened his own chain of northwestern stock companies and moved his family to Australia, where the theater business was booming. When he died seven years later, his wife and children returned to San Francisco, where Blanche received her education in the public schools.

Upon her graduation from college, Blanche became a kindergarten teacher, however, that did not last long. The lure of the theater was too great for the young woman who soon followed in her parents' footsteps.

Miss Bates made her debut in a one-act play at Stockwell's Theatre and was so well received that she joined the Frawly Stock Company, appearing in her first success as Mrs. Hillary in "The Senator."

Blanche Bates was an attractive woman with drive and determination. She played light comedy and drama with a natural spontaneity that charmed San Francisco audiences. Miss Bates was triumphant as Nora in "A Doll's House," the first of Henrik Ibsen's plays to be presented on the West Coast. Ibsen wrote realistic plays about the social problems of the era and was considered to be the father of modern drama.

Following her success in the West, Blanche moved on to New York City, the nation's theater capital, where her talent caught the attention of producer David Belasco. Belasco provided Miss Bates with her first historic role as Cho-Cho San in the original "Madame Butterfly." From there she went on to appear in "The Darling of the Gods," and as Cigarette in "Under Two Flags," a play that made her the idol of New York audiences. The role that made Blanche Bates famous, however, was Minnie Smith in David Belasco's "The Girl of the Golden West." In this play Blanche was given the opportunity to display her fascinating emotional power. Belasco created the character for her, and Blanche played it to perfection; she became known as the girl of the Golden West.

She continued to appear in Belasco's plays for eight years, but eventually became restless. In 1912 Miss Bates married newspaper editor George Creel, and turned her considerable talents to raising children and caring for her home. She continued to live a quiet life, returning to the stage occasionally for the next 16 years, and in 1926 Blanche Bates retired from the theater.

In 1941, at the age of 68, she suffered a stoke and died in her San Francisco home.

*Blanche Bates as Nora in
"The Doll's House."*

Courtesy California State Library

Eva Tanguay,
the "I Don't Care Girl."

EVA TANGUAY

E va Tanguay was a personality songstress of yesterday who catapulted from obscurity to fame, becoming nationally known as the "I Don't Care Girl." She was an expression of the cultural revolution in America around the turn-of-the-century and the antithesis of every middle-class housewife. It was said her exciting career was one of the most colorful in the history of the theater.

Miss Tanguay was born in 1878 in Quebec, Canada, of French-Canadian parents. The family moved to the United States when she was six years old. A few months after the move her father passed away, leaving the family without financial means. When Eva was eight, a juvenile lead became available in a play for the role of Little Lord Fauntleroy. Eva took the part, and through her acting ability the family escaped from poverty to a better life; the girl's education was forgotten. She went on a five-year tour, later moving into small parts in other plays and eventually entering vaudeville.

Although Eva Tanguay lacked talent, her energetic personality, shapely figure, and determination to succeed allowed her to reach the top of her profession. With one of the most expensive publicity and sales buildups of that era, she launched an advertising campaign that moved her from a $250 a week entertainer to a $3,500 a week star. Her drawing power earned repeat performances season after season, and Miss Tanguay became what was considered the highest paid performer in vaudeville. She had no illusions about her talent, however, and would often reply to a compliment by saying she had just been lucky. It has been said Eva's secret lay in her electric personality, which she used to the utmost. Miss Tanguay's tousled hair, ability to command the attention of her audience, and her lavish, beaded costumes proved profitable. One scanty outfit that shocked American audiences was created from dollar bills with Lincoln pennies for spangles. A few of her well-known songs were: "I've Got to Be Crazy,"

"I Want Someone to Go Wild With Me," and "It's All Been Done Before but Not the Way I Do It."

Eva Tanguay was received by her audiences with mixed emotions. She was considered to be vulgar, vital, feminine, and definitely independent. In the role of Sambo Girl, Miss Tanguay briefly became the darling of the theater, and in 1906 "Salome" became her most profitable play.

Miss Tanguay was popular from 1904 through 1915. She was married twice; both marriages failed. Eva never seemed to have a successful private life and found love and security with her family and a few close friends. During her lifetime it has been estimated she earned a fortune, but lost most of it through bad investments and generosity to others.

In 1933 Eva was penniless and became blind. The famous actress Sophie Tucker came to her aid and paid for an operation that restored her sight. Following that, Miss Tanguay made several appearances before retiring to a modest home in Hollywood, California. She lived the rest of her life in seclusion, preferring to be remembered as the carefree "I Don't Care Girl" rather than an aging actress.

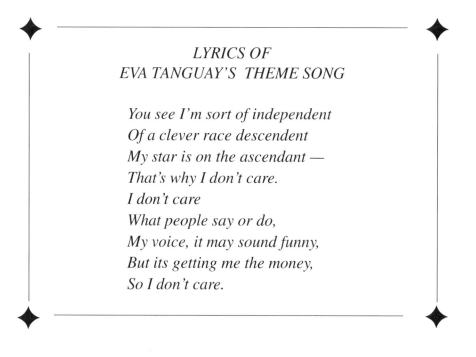

LYRICS OF
EVA TANGUAY'S THEME SONG

You see I'm sort of independent
Of a clever race descendent
My star is on the ascendant —
That's why I don't care.
I don't care
What people say or do,
My voice, it may sound funny,
But its getting me the money,
So I don't care.

BIBLIOGRAPHY

Benson, Ivan, *Mark Twain's Western Years,* 1938

Blum, Daniel A., *A Pictorial History of the American Theatre,* 1971

Brough, James H., *Miss Lillian Russell,* 1978

Brough, James H., *The Prince and the Lily,* 1975

Brown, Dee, *The Gentle Tamers,* 1958

Burke, John, *Duet in Diamonds, 1972*

Creahan, John, *The Life of Laura Keene,* 1897

Falk, Bernard, *The Naked Lady,* 1852 (revised)

Gerson, Noel B., *Because I Loved Him: The Life and Loves of Lillie Langtry,* 1971

Graham, Phillip, *Showboats: The History of An American Institution,* 1951

Gronowicz, Antone, *Modjeska: Her Life and Loves.* 1956

Holdenredge, Helen, *The Woman in Black,* 1955

Hunt, Rockwell D., *California and Californians: The American Period,* 1926

Lesser, Allen, *Enchanting Rebel,* 1949

Lewis, Paul, *Queen of the Plaza; A biography of Adah Isaacs Menken,* 1964

Lyman, George D., *The Saga of the Comstock,* 1934

MacMinn, George R., *The Theatre of the Golden Era in California,* 1941

Mack, Effie, *Mark Twain in Nevada,* 1947

Magoon, Genevieve, *The Story of Guenoc Ranch,* 1976

Maugham, Somerset, *A Writer's Notebook,* 1949

Modjeska, Helena, *Memories and Impressions of Helena Modjeska, an autobiography,* 1910

BIBLIOGRAPHY

Radcliffe College, *Notable Women: a Biographical Dictionary, Volumes One, Two and Three*

Richardson, Warren, *History of the First Frontier Days,   1881*

Rourke, Constance, *Troupers of the Gold Coast,   1928*

Skinner, Cornelia Otis, *Madame Sarah,   1967*

Skinner, Otis, *Footlights and Spotlights: "Recollections of my Life on Stage,   1924*

Strang, Lewis C., *Famous Actresses of the Day,   1899*

Strickland, Dorothy, Laura Keene, *Unpublished Thesis, University of Arizona, 1961*

Wagenknecht, Edward, *Seven Daughters of the Theatre, 1964*

Willis, John, *A Pictorial Revue of the American Theatre, 1971*

MAGAZINES

California Historical Society Quarterly, V. XX1 *"Quand Meme" a few California footnotes to the biography of Sarah Bernhardt,   1942*

Cosmopolitan, *February-September, 1922, Lillian Russell's Reminiscences*

Ladies Home Journal, *March, April, May, 1926, The One I Knew Least of All, by Maude Adams*

Sunset, 1904, *Volume 13, The Lesson of Maude Adams' Success*

Theatre magazine, 1930, *The Romance of Sarah Bernhardt*

ALL NEWSPAPER ARTICLES AND REVIEWS
ARE NOTED WITHIN THE TEXT.

Unfortunately most of the newspaper articles and reviews can no longer be reproduced.